GW01238324

THE BODY
OF CHRIST
AND THE GIFTS

THE BODY
OF CHRIST
AND THE GIFTS

But covet earnestly the
best gifts: and yet show I unto you
a more excellent way
1 Corinthians 12:31

JOHN METCALFE

THE PUBLISHING TRUST
Church road, Tylers Green, Penn, Buckinghamshire

Printed and Published by
The John Metcalfe Publishing Trust
Church Road, Tylers Green
Penn, Buckinghamshire

–

Distributed by Trust Representatives
and Agents world-wide

In the Far East

Bethany, Orchard Point P.O. Box 0373
Singapore 912313

–

© John Metcalfe Publishing Trust 2001
All Rights Reserved

–

First Published 2001

–

ISBN 1 870039 82 3

–

CONTENTS

THE BODY
OF CHRIST
AND THE GIFTS

Introduction

ALTHOUGH the apostle Paul had touched briefly upon the subject of the body of Christ when opening the truth concerning the gifts and baptism of the Spirit, I Corinthians 12:1-13, it is not until the following verses that he applies the figure of the body itself, I Corinthians 12:14-26.

Here he is not at all referring *directly* to the body of Christ. He points to the physical frame, by way of allegory drawing inferences from the relation of one's body to its members, and one's members to that body.

1

However–despite the vast differences–with propriety certain parallels may be drawn between one's own body and its members, and the body of Christ and its members. That is, the inferences drawn in I Corinthians 12:14-26 may in a figure be transferred to the members of the body of Christ, and to that body itself.

Hence, whilst this passage refers to the human frame, because it does so with but one object in mind, at the last the apostle concludes, 'Now ye are the body of Christ, and members in particular', I Corinthians 12:27.

In principle verses 14-26 present two propositions in relation to the body and its members. The first appears in verse 14: 'For the body is not one member, but many.' This proposes *one body but many members*, and is expounded by way of allegory in I Corinthians 12:15-19.

The second proposition is in verse 20: 'But now are they many members, yet but one body.' This shifts the emphasis, declaring *many members yet but one body*. This is opened by similar allegory between verses 21-26.

In the first, Paul argues from the body to the members; in the second, from the members to the body. Although seemingly simple–the members addressing one another–the force of the apostle's propositions, and their respective conclusions, seen aright, comes with powerful impact to the Corinthians. To the contemporary situation in modern-day 'Christianity', the application is absolutely devastating.

I

One Body but Many Members

CONSIDER the first proposition, 'For the body is not one member, but many', I Corinthians 12:14. This postulates *one body but many members*, upon which the apostle enlarges in verses 15-19. This proposition *seems* to state the obvious, but by it the apostle presses home the truth. For by making much more obvious what is natural, he directs them the more diligently to consider the spiritual implications of these things in the body of Christ.

To this end Paul supposes two members of one's body able to deny the purpose of their existence. Showing the folly of this, the apostle questions the denial imagined regarding each member respectively. His questions make the two members' statements appear ludicrous. He concludes this immediate context with the truth of verse 18, and the question of verse 19.

To return to the two questions. These are imagined as being asked by the foot and the ear respectively. Suppose the foot–had

3

it power to speak–should say, 'Because I am not the hand, I am not of the body.' Again, imagine the ear–assuming it could speak–saying, 'Because I am not the eye, I am not of the body.'

But, allowing the licence of the figure, such speech is preposterous. To show *how* preposterous, the apostle dismisses the vanity of such foolish statements by the repeated question, '*Is it therefore not of the body?*'. That is, assuming the foot and the ear, because they are not the hand and the eye, *should* be capable of saying, 'Therefore I am not of the body', I Corinthians 12:15,16.

Just *suppose*–imagines the apostle–these members should so speak: Well, *what difference would it make?* None at all. Speak away with such vain froth: '*Is it therefore not of the body?*' The empty words, light as air, *change nothing in reality*. What these members say, or do not say, does not decide things, or alter anything.

The truth is that both members are what they are because God has created them so. Moreover they are not created to be what they are in order to be independent of the body itself. The member is what it is, not for itself, or for its own sake, but it is what it is for the body, and for the body's sake.

Whence it follows that no member exists for itself: it exists for him whose body it is, into which that member is incorporated. It is *what* it is, and *where* it is, because God has so created the body that each member is exactly what is necessary in the place in which it is set. *That* member would be useless were it set elsewhere. It is created naturally to function–according to its fashion and form–expressly where it has been placed, and placed perfectly in order to realize its full usefulness to the body as a whole.

How suited therefore the figure employed by Paul, imagining two such members to be in the position of speaking, and doing so as severing themselves from the body–if they could–because such members, rejecting their own nature, deny the very purpose of their existence. And for what cause? For this cause: they are neither of the nature nor in the place which they fancy for themselves: then, vexed, they refuse to accept that they are members of the body at all. Are they therefore not of the body?

Then what clamouring members are these? Such presumption arises from considering nothing other than themselves. From questioning, Why am I not this? Or, Why can I not be that? And whining, Well, if I am not *this*; or if I cannot be *that*; then I am not of the body, and disassociate myself from the body. *But is it therefore not of the body?*

Such a member–supposing it could do so–should rather give thanks. And if it were possible that it should ask questions, ask these questions: How can I respond more fully, more efficiently, to him to whose body I belong, so as to please *him*, being what I am? How can I function in harmony and co-ordination with each other member, every one in its proper place and due order, so as to serve him whose members we are?

Thus the purpose for the existence of the members of the body, every one, would be fulfilled. And the reason for the being of each member, unique in its place in the body–in concert with all–would be realized.

But are these inferences, drawn from the members of one's body–and their imaginary speech–suited to the state of the body of Christ at Corinth? They were suited to *correct* that state. For, whatever their condition, still, all had been baptized in one Spirit into one body, and all repented with a repentance not to be repented of–II Corinthians 7:8-11–besides which, all were of the same mind and the same judgment, all spake the same thing, and all were gathered into the unity of the one *ecclesia of God* at Corinth.

But is the state that was at Corinth, which this epistle gener-ally–and that figure of the body particularly–was sent to correct, in any way comparable to the state of the contemporary professing church? No, it is not. There is not the remotest resemblance between the two. They are as far apart as the east is from the west.

Whatever the faults of the Corinthians, they existed within the unity of the only assembly or *ecclesia* in that entire city, and also in all the earth. However the Corinthians might have erred, nevertheless, they *had* all been baptized in one Spirit into one body. No matter how the Corinthians had strayed, they had strayed one from the other, or from the apostle, *within the integrity of the only visible gathering that existed.* That integrity— called into the fellowship of God's Son, into the unity of Father, Son, and Holy Ghost, *manifestly set forth in the ecclesia*—that integrity, I say, remained unbroken.

Contemporary Christianity—in all its forms—is the direct opposite of that original unity, the unity of the one body of Christ. Brethrenism claims—or used to claim—that it is the exception; but this is palpable nonsense: there are more divisions and sects at war with each other in Brethrenism, than there are in those from whom they had separated in order to disintegrate into this splintered and fragmented contradiction of even the semblance of unity. And where is the unity of *one body*—visibly manifested— in that?

As to the rest of Christendom, consisting as it does of numerous denominations, independencies, parties, groups, and sects, each in fact divided from the other; all having their own peculiarities, dogma, and systems; every one with a mixed congregation comprised of believer and unbeliever, the world and the church, light and darkness; the preponderance being for the worst: What of this? This mixed multitude of divisions is as irreconcilable as it is incurable. As prophesied in holy writ, it is irremediable: from it, all that is of God should repent, depart, and cry for the unity of *one* body.

Then can they agree in nothing? Yes, they can agree in two things. First, they can agree to tolerate this evil which, together, they embody, saying nothing whatsoever about it, either in their own party, or in that of others. Second, they can agree in their divided entities stoutly to defend the *status quo*, and this alike by utterly shutting their eyes and ears to the least sight or the faintest sound of the truth of God's *ecclesia* as it was in the beginning, is now, and ever shall be: O, tacitly they can agree together wholly to ignore the truth of the one body *of Christ*!

Yet even this, so-called 'evangelicals' will justify in their iniquity, claiming that the body is invisible; that its members are scattered like so many indiscernible ghosts; that they merge imperceptibly each one among and with the worldly, divided, invented, disobedient divisions of Christendom; that they abide wraith-like–unknown, unseen, unaware, uncomprehending– invisible amidst the membership of unbelieving congregations. And this is the unity of one body? Oh, yes, they say, and 'Bishop' Ryle saith it: and who is this Disraeli-appointed Ryle to overturn the everlasting gospel?

Ah, but, says the evangelical, the body is hidden in the professing church. But it is not a church: it is a series of disparate denominations, sects, independencies and divisions. And it is not a profession: for if there is one thing that they do *not* hold, nor will they ever profess, it is the faith once delivered to the saints.

And of all the contradictions in terms, none is so farcically blatant as the absurdity of the words 'an invisible body'. An invisible body is no body at all: it is a spirit. 'Know ye not that your *bodies* are the members of Christ?', I Corinthians 6:15. *Inwardly* those baptized in one Spirit are united in one; yes: but also *outwardly* those spiritually in union are likewise united *in one body*. Its unity is *visible*. You can see it. If not, it is no body.

But the truth is, 'evangelicals' dare not admit what stares them in the face: the body of Christ is a reality in the word of God, and in the Spirit of truth, from which they have utterly

7

fallen, so that *it no longer appears*. What appears is that like the Pharisees of old 'these are they that justify themselves'. Yes, and in so doing, condemn the preciousness of the body of Christ to the Head. If not, let them admit of it, and confess and forsake their sin.

Let them be like the Jewish remnant according to the election of grace, which, as one man, repented at the preaching of John, and, openly confessing their sins, were baptized of him in Jordan. Let them heed the cry, 'Come out of her, my people'. Let them cleanse themselves from all filthiness of the flesh and spirit. Let them 'come out from among them, and be separate'. Let them go forth unto Christ *without the camp*. They will not find themselves alone.

So has the Spirit been grieved in the past, and in this present generation, in which we and our fathers have sinned, that his divine influences have been well-nigh withdrawn, and in their place a lying spirit with his fleshly incitements has deluded multitudes. And since they would not receive the love of the truth, God has given them over to their delusions. Nevertheless, to the remnant that is left, a voice cries in the wilderness.

We who are of this remnant are to repent, and return, and be united in one Spirit–for 'there is one body, and one Spirit, even as ye are called in one hope of your calling'–that it may appear again that the body of Christ is a reality, so that the world may know that the Father sent the Son; and know it, precisely because of this reality of fellowship–the apostles' fellowship–in Father, Son, and Holy Ghost.

And should it be that there are those who have repented in a place, and received the truth: let them not suppose that we fulfil all the mind of the Lord, till we in every place are so united. Thus not only do we manifest the unity of the Spirit among the members of the one body of Christ in the *ecclesia* in which we are called; but also in all the earth–in demonstration of the Spirit and of power – we show forth as one this unity, under the Head, of the whole body, the one *ecclesia*.

This is that, in the light and to the realization of which by the Spirit, we are called, and to which we should come with heart-broken penitence, with mourning and humility, for the failure and sin of which we and our fathers have been the cause.

Till we are fully returned to this – not only in a given locality; but in the unity of *one* body throughout the whole earth, of all who are so met in every place – we declare, in practice, however we delude ourselves in theory, 'Because I am not the hand, I am not of the body'. And again – for in the mouth of two or three witnesses every matter is established – 'Because I am not the eye, I am not of the body'. But if God hath wrought at all in thee, Art thou not of the body?

To assert independence from the one body of Christ – so as to join ourselves in the sin of schism with what *must* be infinitely less – is, in effect, by one's life, volition, and direction, to deny both the body of Christ, and that one is a member of that body. Independence of the body therefore is as impossible to true members, as it is to the real members of one's own body. If not, what does the figure, and what does the passage, mean?

How this shows up the Charismatic delusion – among others – in which, claiming the baptism of the Spirit, supposing to seal that claim by the twofold extravagance of the loss of self-control on the one hand, and the pretence to 'signs' – such as gibberish – on the other, these impostors *eschew the body of Christ, properly so-called.* Do they not? Are they not found, gleefully expressing themselves, united with their congregations, whether in Roman Catholic, Anglican, Nonconformist, Brethren, Independent, Group, or House-meeting?

I Corinthians 12:17 demonstrates by two simple questions the indispensability of many members in one body. This appears in the necessity of many needed – but quite different – functions.

To these functions, respectively, the members correspond; for them, as a whole, they were created, and do exist. Hence the irony of Paul's two rhetorical questions.

'If the whole body were an eye, where were'—*the function of*—'hearing?' *That* function, necessitates an *ear*. And only the corresponding member can perform the required function. How essential then, the variety, co-ordination, and unity of the members to the body. How can—with the wildest imagination—the whole body be an eye? How can it be a body unto itself?

And whilst asserting its independency, will it yet have the temerity to profess that it—so mean, so small, not to say dis-obedient, a member—is sufficient for the Head of the body to indwell, that *thus* he might fully express *himself*? What presump-tuous folly! *A man cannot express himself through an eye only.* A man is so constituted that he needs every member of his body for full self-expression.

One can *see* through an eye: it *is* an essential *part* of self-expression: but *only* a part. It requires *all* the parts, every member, the whole of the functions, working together as one under the direction of the head, in order that a person should achieve self-expression.

Any one member, any single function, is *not* an expression, but only a part, a contributory function, of the full expression. He whose body it is requires the co-ordinated unity of the whole range of functions from every member, enlivened together in harmony, to express the fulness of his personality who indwells the whole.

Hence the irony of Paul's question: as if one member were—or possibly could be—the whole body. The very idea is at once grotesque, fantastic, and repellent. One member can never be the body, much less a body unto itself. Yet 'evangelicals' have for generations acted *in practice* upon the presumption that it is so.

Is it any wonder that ICHABOD is written over our portals, and that, in wrath, the *presence of* God has departed from us, after *so long* a time of patient longsuffering, of enduring our inventions, to see if at last our fathers or we might come to repentance and reformation?

In the same verse–I Corinthians 12:17–the apostle, as if to call another witness against such a gross impossibility, repeats the question in terms of the faculty of hearing: 'If the whole body were'–no more than the faculty of–'hearing, where were the'– faculty of–'smelling?' The absurd folly of such a proposition in nature, though ludicrous, serves a vital purpose: by giving voice to the inanity of the very idea in natural things, Paul presses home the truth that such an aberration were even more shocking in spiritual things.

As if any one member could so bloat itself as to eclipse all the others, making out that nothing signifies save *this* member!

Would not he whose body it is–allowing of the figure used by Paul–say to it, What doest thou? But if it replied, I am here to express your lordship over me! What would be the rejoinder but this: Thou fool! Am I so small in thy sight? I need you; but I need *every other member with you.* I need your function; but I need *every other member to function in harmony also*: only *thus* am I expressed.

'So also is the Christ', I Corinthians 12:12.

That is, just as 'God hath set the members *every one of them* in the body, as it hath pleased him', I Corinthians 12:18, 'so also is the Christ'. However, strictly–except by allusion–verse 18 does not refer to the body of Christ, but to the body of man in the creation.

Then how could such a creation, both in its parts, and in the sum of those parts, be other than 'very good', so that 'God *rested* on the seventh day from all his work which he had made'?

Then, consistent with God's nature, his rest, and his own image, man reflected, down to the very least member, the divine perfection of the work of him who set every member in the body, as it pleased him.

Wherefore observe that, *firstly*, it hath pleased God perfectly to form each member so that it is ideally adapted to perform its function; *secondly*, that all the members–whether paired or single–are set in that place in the body admirably suited–in concert with every other member–to its use; *thirdly*, that–save for pairs: as hands, eyes, or ears, for example–each member is essential for that distinctive use for which it, alone, was created and set in the body; and *fourthly*, that God hath set all together, each in its respective place, so that the whole body, perfectly synchronized and harmoniously responsive, answers to the head, according to the volition and will of him whose body it is, to the glory of God.

This end and result of the creation of the body of man, and this setting of the members of that body so agreeably in concert with perfect efficiency of movement and energy, is what is called 'as it hath pleased him'. For what pleases God is order, perfection, harmony, subjection, and beauty. Thus the members set in the body were 'as it hath pleased him', and, viewing his work in creation, it gave to God such pleasure that it is written, 'behold, it was very good'.

And if this be so with the creation and setting of the members of the body of man, shall it be *less so* with the members of the body of Christ? My brethren, these things ought not to be. Then why is it that the holy apostle is obliged thus to write?

'And if they were all one member, where were the body?', I Corinthians 12:19. This verse concludes the first proposition of the apostle, namely, *one body but many members*. What a conclusion! What? Must the apostle needs conclude such a proposition with the words, 'And if they were all one member, where were the body?'. Yes, for shame, he must.

Irrespective of what member and function was bestowed upon those at Corinth, what was it that each actually usurped to himself—or, for shame, herself—in their assembling together? What was it that made them appear 'all one member', so that the mentally sound unbeliever should declare them to be mad? What was it? It was that they were all tongues. They '*all* spoke with tongues', and, it appears, all at once, I Corinthians 14:23. Then, 'Where were the body?'

And this, remark, during the lifetime of the apostles, in an apostolic age when it was granted to them, and to the *ecclesia* raised up under their authority, to show forth such signs and wonders, as in parallel at the commencement with Israel.

Yet, even in such auspicious apostolic beginnings of the *ecclesia*, these very same early miraculous signs evidently were what the Corinthians abused, both in the apparently mad bedlam of their assembling, and in their usurping what was in fact 'a sign, not to them that believe, but to them that believe not', I Corinthians 14:22.

And this, I say, in a day when such signs *were* given, under the safe hands of the apostles, to indicate to the whole world, and the entire age, *God's* inauguration of the new testament, and his bringing in of the body of Christ at the beginning.

II

Many Members yet but One Body

VERSE 19 concludes the apostle's first proposition, *one body, but many members*, I Corinthians 12:14, which he expounds between verses 15-19. It also leads naturally to his second proposition, which follows immediately, namely, *many members, yet but one body*, I Corinthians 12:20, the opening of which appears in verses 21-26.

In the first case Paul had argued from the body to the members. The body embraced all the members. They were all members, which, together, constituted that body. The number of the members, the variety of their functions, the diversity of their appearance, made no difference to – in fact, it conspired to enhance – the truth of the one body.

That is the emphasis of the divergence of so numerous yet distinct a conjunction of members: *together* – and they *are* together –

they constitute one body. 'One body but many members.' Thus the difference and variety of the many members *stress*, not *contradict*, the unity of the body, I Corinthians 12:14-19.

Although the alteration of the emphasis in the second proposition may appear so slight that it seems a distinction without a difference, obviously this cannot be so: rather, it should be clear immediately that such a weighty matter must be considered from every aspect, and in each nuance of meaning.

Then, it is emphatically and distinctly true that it behoves the apostle now to stress that *there are many members, yet but one body*, I Corinthians 12:20, where Paul argues not from the body to the many members, *but from the many members to the one body.* Consider this.

The members have 'need' one of the other in the one body. This word 'need' appears twice, verse 21. Likewise the members have a 'necessity' each one of the other, in the nature of the one body, verse 22. *That* is the issue in these verses: the *need*; the *necessity*; namely, *the need, the necessity of every member to the whole body.* That is what Paul feels compelled to impress upon the Corinthians.

The fact of varied members, of their differing characteristics, of their distinct nature, of their diverse function, of their unique appearance, *cannot disassociate those members from the one body.* Whatever their differences, each and all belong to the body, and *to nothing else but the body.*

The very idea of severance from the body as if to operate in connection with some alternative organism – much less organisation – is an impossibility in nature, a transgression against creation, and a grotesque parody of all that is lawful, proper and orderly.

Yet has not this concept become the norm in the organisations, systems, denominations, societies, schools, 'charities', and other superfluous growths and cancers of modern Christendom? As if the members *could* be considered in connection with anything other than the one body? For there is but *one* body.

But Christendom, in its nature, stands in a multitude of independent structures, not one of which existed in the new testament. None of this can possibly be justified by holy scripture, which declares with categorical emphasis–however many or diverse the true and living members –'yet but *one body*', I Corinthians 12:20.

Whence it follows that no function can be exercised by any member independent of the one body. Nothing else exists to those members *but* one body. All members, however varied; all functions, notwithstanding their diversity; *pertain exclusively to the one body.*

No other organism –much less organisation– exists to the members save that one corporate entity of him whose body it is. All the members are of that one body, whether great or small, weak or strong; often or little used: '*yet but one body.*'

As in the first proposition the apostle again supposes, for the sake of argument, that one member might ask hypothetical questions or make theoretical statements to another. Specifically, the eye to the hand, or the head to the feet.

But, there being '*yet but one body*', these members *cannot* make such impossible hypothetical statements as this: 'I have no need of you.' They have *every* need of each other, and, vastly more important, the body itself has the utmost necessity of all the members, none excluded.

The eye say to the hand, I have no need of thee? But the hand is of the utmost necessity to the eye, otherwise, what is *seen* cannot be put to *use*. Why not? Because the eye is not a hand. The eye which sees, requires the hand which works.

Besides, transcending the hypothesis, What is this, that the members speak of themselves with such presumptuous impudence? It is for *him whose body it is, whose members these are*, to speak, or not to speak; to direct, or not to direct, every single one according to his own will.

The whole is one co-ordinated organism for the self-expression of him whose body it is: then what is this height of arrogance–given the figure–that the members dare to speak–much less to act–as if they were each detached bodies in and of themselves?

The head say to the feet, I have no need of you? But the head can neither stand nor can it proceed in motion without the feet. The feet cannot function as the head, nor can the head fulfil its purpose without the feet.

Both head and feet act in concord, not to do the work of the whole body, but to function as unique and diverse members of that body, so that the entire body, with *every* member, may give due expression to the personality of him to whom all belongs as one. Without this, there *is* no body: only dismemberment.

Next, making a further comparison between the members of one's body, Paul speaks of differences of another sort: some are 'feeble'; others 'uncomely'. That is, relative to those which appear 'honourable', or 'more comely'.

What of this? Does this make them less members than the others, or of meaner value? Can this be a cause of one despising another, or of some rejecting those held by them to be inferior? God forbid: else where were the body's unity? or of what use are such disjointed and contradictory members to the person whose body it is?

'Nay, much more those members of the body, which seem to be more feeble, are necessary: and those members of the body, which we think to be less honourable, upon these we bestow more abundant honour; and our uncomely parts have more abundant comeliness.

'For our comely parts have no need: but God hath tempered the body together, having given more abundant honour to that part which lacked: that there should be no schism in the body; but that the members should have the same care one for another.

'And whether one member suffer, all the members suffer with it; or one member be honoured, all the members rejoice with it. Now ye are the body of Christ, and members in particular', I Corinthians 12:22-27.

By 'feeble' the apostle refers to those members which are especially vulnerable, lacking natural protection. For example, the eye: how sensitive, how susceptible to injury – in a word, feeble – this member appears. Then, every member instinctively moves to guard and protect such a member in case of danger.

The same applies to the ear, should some foreign matter threaten this orifice: the head flinches, the hand flies to defend the vulnerable and exposed member, and the feet run from the area of danger.

Thus nature itself teaches – and instinctive reaction instructs – that all the members of the body as one fly to the protection of those members weaker than themselves. Every member by a kind of natural reflex hastens to defend and strengthen that which is more feeble, thus bestowing 'more abundant honour', because 'all the members' have 'the same care one for another'.

Now Paul draws attention to another relative difference between the members of the body: some are 'uncomely', whereas certain others are 'comely'. But should this be the cause of 'schism in the body' according to nature? Certainly not. Once more, nature itself teaches quite the opposite.

An 'uncomely' member is one not prepossessing in sight. Yet upon these also we bestow 'more abundant honour'. For example, the feet. Hardly the most attractive members, these might well be considered 'uncomely'. Yet, especially in Paul's day, and in other parts of the world to this day, though less honourable, upon these it is at once natural, necessary, and courteous to bestow special attention.

John the Baptist considered himself unworthy so much as to unloose the latchet of the Lord's shoes, let alone wash his feet. Simon the Pharisee, however, disdained even – at the least – to provide the expected water for the Lord to wash his own feet when entering the house. For, said Jesus, 'thou gavest me no water for my feet', Luke 7:44.

The Lord himself washed the disciples' feet, much to the consternation of Peter, who considered it utterly beneath the Lord to wash the feet of one as unfit as himself. Indeed–much like to John the Baptist–far from having *his* feet washed, he thought it unworthy in himself so much as to attempt to wash the *Lord's* feet: 'And shalt *thou* wash *my* feet?'

Where, in those days of open shoes or sandals, before entering the house it was considered both proper and decent to wash the feet: to bestow honour, that is, on one's own or others' uncomely members. Whence it appears that thus to bestow honour upon the uncomely members was universal in practice.

Hence the suitability of the apostle's application, I Corinthians 12:23, for the hands serve, the eyes guide, and the joints supply, as one bends to wash and cleanse these lowliest and least comely of members. That is, *every other member* combines in recognition of the significance of *these*, in and to the *whole* body, notwithstanding their uncomeliness!

From this point Paul begins to apply lessons from the figure of the body to the members of the body of Christ with much more direct and pointed attention. For example, the use of the word 'schism', I Corinthians 12:25, a word impossible to apply accurately to one's own body, but tragically applicable to the members of the body of Christ.

But God has tempered – bound, given cohesion, compounded, blended – the body together, 'that there should be no schism in the body'. The Greek *schisma*, or *schizō*, has been rendered 'division; rent; schism'; or 'break; divide; rend; open'.

This indicates a rent, cleft, or division. Now, this cannot refer to the body naturally, for in such a case it would imply amputation; dismemberment; severance; or mutilation.

Then Paul is applying the word *schisma* to the members of the body of Christ spiritually. It is a direct application. The apostle means that in the body of Christ, wherever found, such is the work of God in 'tempering' the members of the body together, *that in consequence there should be* – or, one might say, *there could be* – *no schism.*

On the contrary, because of the Father, the Son, and the Holy Ghost, all 'the members should have the same care one for another', I Corinthians 12:25, 'that there should be no schism in the body'.

'And whether one member suffer, all the members suffer with it.' In effect, as it is true of one's own body, this is fulfilled in the body of Christ. If the eye or ear be afflicted, or should some laceration or severe bruising affect a part, such is the pain of that single member that one's whole body seems to be nothing but that member! Namely 'all the members suffer with it', until the suffering be eased, and healing finally takes place.

'Or one member be honoured, all the members rejoice with it.' Here the apostle barely waits to give the figure, but with it proceeds immediately to the application. For hardly will a member of one's own body be 'honoured'; yet, certainly, this may be true of a member of the body of Christ.

Nevertheless when excellence is performed by the hand at work, or by the feet in running, or else the eye in sharpness of vision, then it is true that a sense of well-being and of satisfaction floods the whole body.

So when a member of the body of Christ excels in the things of the Lord, and in the work of God, or in spiritual matters, far from envy, disparagement, or sour jealousy being the result, *in the body of Christ*, every single member as it were glows with pleasure and satisfaction at the grace manifested in that member.

How is this love so wonderfully fulfilled? Because 'now are they many members, *yet but one body*.' Whereas in the organisations of religion after the flesh, at the excellence or being honoured of one, the rest of the dead congregation rather give place to 'hatred, variance, emulations, wrath, strife, seditions, heresies, envyings', Galatians 5:20,21.

And why is this? Because it is as Christ said, 'He that gathereth not with me scattereth'. And, because the invention of these divisions is after the flesh, the works of the flesh they will do. Hence such reactions are inevitable in those carnal assemblies which—for all their loud claims and professions from the bible—stand in nothing but the works of man under the dead letter.

Whereas the love of God is shed abroad in the hearts of those who are of him made members of the one body of Christ. Christ fills the body, and his light, life, and love are made manifest in each member, and all the members together as one, having been baptized in one Spirit into one body.

And seeing that this body is of Christ, what life other than his should appear in the members of that body? Then, when one member is honoured, grace reigns, humility rules, love triumphs, and all the members rejoice with it together as one. For 'ye *are* the body of Christ, and members in particular', I Corinthians 12:27.

This verse concludes the entire passage—I Corinthians 12:14-27—in which, under two propositions, the apostle demonstrates the analogy between one's own body, and that of the body of Christ. He had argued first from the relation of the members to the body, and last, from that of the body to the members, concluding the whole with the plain statement 'Now *ye* are the body of Christ, and members in particular'.

However from this point onward to the end of the chapter, Paul begins to open a mystery not previously mentioned, and to reveal the existence of gifts other than those of the Spirit bestowed upon the members of the body of Christ, about which he had spoken hitherto.

Furthermore, to clarify the difference, he also shows the relationship between that which he *had* expounded in I Corinthians 12:7-27, and that which he is *about* to reveal between verses 28-31, the closing verses of this chapter.

III

Gifts of Christ; Gifts of the Spirit

THE apostle commences, 'And God hath set some in the church'– or, rather, 'God hath set certain in the *ecclesia*'– I Corinthians 12:28. Carefully note the change in Paul's description.

Observe that the words 'hath God set' had been used of the members in the body: 'But now *hath God set* the members every one of them in the body, as it hath pleased him', I Corinthians 12:18. Next mark that in verse 28 the apostle repeats the words 'God hath set', not now concerning all the members of the body, but rather 'some'– or 'certain'– whom 'God hath set' *in the ecclesia*: 'And *God hath set* some in *the church*', I Corinthians 12:28.

Yes, but why *repeat* the expression, 'God hath set'? Why change the former reference to 'the members', to the latter expression, namely, to 'some', or rather 'certain', pointing elsewhere? And why is Paul firstly *inclusive* of the members, embracing *all* the members, verse 18, then secondly *exclusive* in relation to 'certain', that is, to 'some' only, verse 28?

23

And why does the first reference state 'in the body', verse 18; whereas the second—to the contrary—affirms specifically 'in the church', verse 28?

First, Why are certain said to be set in the *ecclesia*, verse 28? Elementary: because they are not said to be set in the body.

Why are the members said to be set in the *body*, verse 18? Elementary: because they are not said to be set in the *ecclesia*.

It is simply a question of discerning the mind of the Spirit, and of observing the distinctions in the counsels of God.

Then, whilst *God's setting them*, respectively, is descriptive of the same operation of God, *the wording of the Spirit is such that the same operation is applied twice.*

It is a twofold operation, and the reason is *that it pertains to two different spheres, and concerns two distinct kinds of gifts.* Without discerning this, without observing the distinction, all is confusion. With the discernment, given the observation, everything becomes clear.

Hence observe that every member is said to be set in the body. Likewise mark that only 'some'—*certain*—*persons* are said to be set in the *ecclesia*. These persons are, respectively, 'first apostles, secondarily prophets, thirdly teachers', verse 28.

'After that'—mark well: *after* that—a different matter entirely is mentioned, and mentioned in order to show *the contrast.* That is why it is brought in: 'After that miracles'—this should be, *powers*—'then gifts'—plural: *charismata*—'of healings, helps, governments, diversities of tongues.'

Now these are not *persons*, as was the former case: these are objective gifts. No person is said to possess them: it is simply a formal list of *charismata*, not said to have been personified at all: it is merely objective. Why? *To show the contrast 'After that'.*

After what? After the *persons* whom God hath set in the *ecclesia*, verse 28.

Whereas the apostle *had* been speaking of the body–whether the figure of the body, or the body of Christ itself–this referred to the body and its members *as manifested at Corinth*. There is one body, and *that* is what is brought to light wherever the saints are gathered in the baptism of the Spirit. Then, *there* the one body is distinctively apparent, according to the manifold wisdom of God. In *this* case, at Corinth.

But now in verse 28 *the apostle is no longer speaking of the body of Christ at Corinth, nor of its members, neither yet of the charismata bestowed upon them in the gift of that Spirit who, himself, in person, fills the body.* Now the apostle is speaking of another realm, far wider than that of the body at Corinth, and of other gifts, of far more profound import than the *charismata*.

That is, he is speaking of the *entire ecclesia*, and of those persons whom God hath set in such a realm as this. Thereupon Paul introduces another class of gifts altogether, not previously mentioned.

That is why the apostle repeats the words 'God hath set', verses 18 and 28.

Note the words. First, they are uttered to emphasize that this is the work of God: 'God hath set ... as it hath pleased *him*', verse 18. *Him*, notice. Then this is nothing to do with *man*: this is altogether to do with *the operation of God*.

All the attempts of man–and these are many and various–to copy the work of God and the operation of his hands begin and end in shame, disgrace, and departure, a hollow charade which mocks man's inability to his face. The work of God is inimitable, transcendent, divine: 'God hath set.' It is all of God's initiative, and wholly of the power of God. It is *in this* that his presence is known.

But I return to the question: Why repeat the clause of verse 18 in verse 28? Because the apostle in his doctrine wishes to make clear that *what* God hath set in the first instance is entirely distinct from *what* he hath set in the second.

He sets entirely different things; but the sovereign operation, the divine initiative, the power of God in his work of 'setting'– as such–is the same: that is, the same work of God, twice put forth, inaugurates two different effects.

However the repetition of verse 18 in verse 28 is worded in such a way that we cannot fail to grasp this vital distinction: *The same kind of operation of God actually respects two entirely different things*. That is why in the first case 'God hath set' the members in the body; and in the second, that 'God hath set' certain chosen persons in the *ecclesia*.

So that what God hath set in the body at Corinth *is another thing altogether* than that which God hath set in the *ecclesia* at large.

From which it follows that there are two quite distinct realms of divine operation, and that there are two entirely different classes of gifts.

'God hath set some in the church'–or, rather, I repeat, 'hath set certain in the *ecclesia*'– 'first apostles, secondarily prophets, thirdly teachers.' 'After that' it is another question altogether, the exposition of which must be deferred until it is clearly understood what is meant by 'certain in the *ecclesia*'.

First apostles. In fact, these gifts–for the eleven, together with Paul, the twelfth, are *themselves* the gifts–*preceded* the church, or the *ecclesia*. They were chosen, called, prepared, and sent *in order to bring in the church or ecclesia*.

That choice, calling, preparation, and sending were all things completed *before* they began preaching, in consequence of which those saved were thus constituted God's assembly on earth.

26

So it was when the apostles continued to preach and teach the word of life: 'the Lord added to the church daily such as should be saved.' But, like Paul with the Gentiles, *their apostleship preceded the raising up of the ecclesia.*

Then what comparison can *these*–whose persons *are* the gift– I say, what comparison can these have with the *charismata*? Obviously, they are *another kind of gift altogether.*

They are not members of the body to whom a gift–*charisma*– has been given. They are *themselves* the gift sent before either *ecclesia* or body were called into existence under their ministry.

Then what of 'secondarily prophets, thirdly teachers'? These are gifts in themselves sent to labour under the apostles, either to accompany them, or to establish and extend their work together with them. No wonder a different word is used for such gifts as these, whether apostles, prophets, or teachers.

Paul here refers to the *domata*, first of all the twelve apostolic eyewitnesses, then, in due order, certain others, all alike being regarded as having been sent from the Lord in glory, to call out, increase, and establish the *ecclesia* of God, the body of Christ. Only *after* that, come gifts in the body, namely, the *charismata*.

The 'some' or 'certain', verse 28–individually *doma*, collectively *domata*–are gifts personified: they have an office in virtue of their persons. Their persons *are* the gifts, and that described in terms of their office: first apostles, secondarily prophets, thirdly teachers.

But the members of the body have not an office: *they* are given a gift. Such gifts, *charismata*, are given to their persons, as members of the body. *They* are not the gifts; these gifts of the Spirit are given to *them*. These gifts are things given to persons, namely, to the members of the body of Christ.

Hence, of God, by the Spirit, *charismata* are things persons are enabled to do; what they are gifted to do, as members of the one body of Christ.

The *domata*, however, are *the persons* sent by Christ to raise up the church, or *ecclesia*, before as yet it had existence; or else to establish and extend it, once called into being by the apostolic ministry.

Hence, considering the *ecclesia* either in a view of its being called into existence, or as having been gathered by the saving truth of the evangel, *the actual persons* used of God, sent of Christ, and anointed by the Spirit to do this work, are themselves the gifts, that is, the *domata*. They are the gift of Christ to the *ecclesia* as a whole, hence it is said, 'God hath set certain in the *ecclesia*, first apostles, secondarily prophets, thirdly teachers.'

The apostle continues, 'After that'. After what? After *those* unique, distinct gifts *of chosen persons*, there are other gifts—not sent to the *ecclesia* at large, but still *in* it: for, to the Corinthians, the body and the *ecclesia*, and the *ecclesia* and the body, were both identified at Corinth—other gifts that is, given to every one of the members of the body of Christ, here considered as the assembled Corinthian saints.

These gifts were the *charismata*, of which Paul—having indicated three distinct *doma*—now—'*after this*'—lists five *charisma*, namely powers; gifts of healing; helps; governments; and diversities of tongues.

Note that of these *charismata*, verse 28, the apostle adds two which were omitted in the previous list of nine mentioned in I Corinthians 12:8-10.

What is the difference between *charismata* and *domata*?

Charismata are gifts given *in* the body; *domata* are gifts given *to* the body. *Charismata* are raised up by the Spirit below; *domata* are sent down from Christ above. *Charismata* are gifts given to every member of the body; *domata* are persons given to edify the whole body.

Charismata function in the manifestation of the body in a given place. *Domata* minister to each manifestation of the body in every place. *Charismata* are gifts of the Spirit raised up *in* the body on earth; *Domata* are ministers of Christ sent down from heaven *to* the body on earth.

But quite rightly the question will be pressed, since *charisma* and *doma* have alike been translated 'gift' in English, What is the difference in the Greek? Where is the distinction between the two *Greek* words?

There is a distinction, and I will indicate it; but, first, it must be said that the distinction is a subtle one. So much so that what matters most is not the difference in meaning between the two Greek words, *but that to which the apostle reserves the use of each one respectively, either to the gifts of the Spirit on earth on the one hand, or those of the Son of God from heaven on the other.*

The first of these two Greek words is set apart to indicate the gifts of the Spirit raised up on earth and bestowed upon all the members of the body of Christ in any given place. The second Greek word is retained in order to describe the gifts sent down from heaven by Christ ascended into the glory: gifts, that is, limited to those ministers whom he himself chooses, calls, prepares, and sends.

Sends? Yes, sends from the glory of heaven, for the perfecting of the saints, for the work of the ministry, and for the edifying of the body of Christ in every place, and throughout the age, commencing with the unique foundation of the twelve apostles.

Both *domata* and *charismata* belong – respectively – to large families of words having several branches, each family possessing its own distinct root.

This becomes apparently complicated not only by a similarity of use between the two families, but in some branches by a cross usage resulting in duplication when describing one and the same thing.

Then, in certain cases, whilst there may be a distinction in wording, the fact that certain of these words are used alternately for the same purpose gives the appearance of a distinction without a difference.

Not so, however, with the use of that particular branch – springing from the root – indicated by the word *domata*; nor yet with the analogous *charismata*, developed in turn from its own distinctive origins.

Here, clearly and precisely, there is a consistent difference between that which is reserved for the gifts of Christ *to* the body, and that set apart to describe the gifts of the Spirit *in* the body.

Entire sects have been formed over – what was in fact – the misapplication of the one to the exclusion of the other.

For example, inciting every person, irrespective of the Spirit, to attempt that for which not one was gifted – *the meanwhile quite dismissing the office of minister, as indicated by the word domata* – the Brethren suppose themselves to be 'scriptural', on the basis of their ignorant assumptions from I Corinthians 12:7-27 and 14:26-35; likewise Romans 12:4-8.

Here is nothing other than sheer – indeed, breath-taking – presumption concerning *charismata*, whilst remaining contemptuously dismissive of *domata*. If *this* is not ignorance concerning spiritual – not to say doctrinal and experimental – things, What is?

On the other hand there exist the various priestly, clerical, and pastoral systems, in which one salaried person, 'ordained' by a particular party to take pre-eminence over everyone else –

however gifted–on no basis other than honour received from the respective ministerial education scheme peculiar to his– or her!–given sect or denomination.

Yet these diverse parties vehemently agree as one man to presume to justify this gross aberration on the ground of their misapplication–or *is* it *merely* misapplication?–of the word *domata*, quite blotting out the very memory of the existence of the truth of the *charismata*.

However, to return to the question of the precise meaning of the two words, it is certainly true that this calls for a fine distinction. It is equally true, however, that the greater signific- ance lies in the restraint of the Spirit in each particular context, as a result of which the words *charismata* and *domata* are reserved to indicate the gifts of the Spirit in the body on earth, or the gifts of Christ from the glory, respectively.

As to the actual distinction between the two Greek words in and of themselves, *Charisma* is a gift which points to the disposition of the giver. It *is* a gift, but one which *as such* reflects the benevolent character and bounteous nature of the *giver*.

On the other hand *Doma* emphasizes the gift *itself*. *What* it is that is given. The gift is free, unmerited, and unsought. It is at once generous and magnanimous. The Greek word indicates a gratuitous present.

Although neither the singular *doma* nor the plural *domata* appear in the text of I Corinthians 12, nevertheless what the word describes–and for which it is duly reserved–*does* appear, and it is this that should be observed as of the greater significance.

Then where does that which *domata* describes appear? In the verse in question: 'God hath set certain in the *ecclesia*, first apostles, secondarily prophets, thirdly teachers', I Corinthians 12:28.

Nevertheless, the *burden* of the apostle in First Corinthians lies in his describing the *charismata*, not in indicating the *domata*. That is why—of all the epistles—this truth occupies so large a part, unmatched elsewhere in the new testament, although it is true that Romans 12:4-8 contributes considerably to the revelation of the mind of the Spirit concerning such charismatic gifts.

Just so, the revelation of the *domata* appears to be concentrated in one book in particular, namely, the Epistle to the Ephesians. Nevertheless, as with *charismata* and the Romans, likewise the four evangelists—Matthew, Mark, Luke, and John—together with the Pastoral Epistles, contribute greatly to what is revealed concerning the *domata*.

And this is not to mention the Acts of the Apostles—of the *apostles*, note—and other places in which what is sent down and given from the Son of God in heaven—despite that the Greek word itself may not actually appear in the text—*show* the wonderful kindness and work of the Lord from the glory in sending those rare and choice gifts, his own sent ministers.

IV

Christ's descent; ascent; and the Gifts

THE apostle points clearly and definitively to the δόματα, *domata*, in Ephesians 4:8; 'Wherefore he saith, When he ascended up on high, he led captivity captive, and gave gifts unto men.' These gifts are the *domata*: 'first apostles, secondarily prophets, thirdly teachers', I Corinthians 12:28, compare Ephesians 4:11.

The immediate context of Ephesians 4:8 may seem to present difficulties to the reader, but in fact it greatly supports the truth which the apostle is about to open. 'But unto every one of us is given grace according to the measure of the gift of Christ', Ephesians 4:7. As in the case of Ephesians 3:7, this verse utilises the related Greek word δωρεά, *dōrea*.

Complexities arise from the assumption that 'every one of us', Ephesians 4:7, refers to all saints. It does not. It refers to the *domata*, those chosen out from all saints to be the ministers of Christ to them. Were the pronouns in this context to be observed,

33

all difficulties would be resolved. Then the verse would appear to substantiate, not vitiate, Ephesians 4:8.

The apostle spoke of 'I' as opposed to 'you', verse 1. He had spoken of 'the body'; of 'ye'; of 'your'; verse 4. Again, he referred to 'all', namely, 'in *you* all', verse 6. *Then* he said 'But'. That is, *in contrast*, verse 7, '*But* unto every one of *us*.' Us? Us in contrast with whom? With you. 'But every one of *us*', verse 7, in contrast with '*you* all', verse 6.

If not, Why change the pronouns? If not, why contrast the verses? If not, why does the apostle limit the measure of 'the gift of Christ' to the *domata*, verse 7, as opposed to his having expanded 'the gifts of the Spirit' to the whole body, verse 4?

If not, why does the apostle proceed immediately to extend verse 7 with the 'Wherefore' of verse 8, which, without question, speaks of the *domata* sent in the gift of Christ *to* all saints, that is, *to* the body?

It follows, it must follow, verse 7 is *inclusive* of every one of the *domata*, whatever the respective measure of the gift of Christ – ascended – in each. Whence it is evident that verse 7 must be *exclusive* of the body and its members, to whom and for whom each *doma* is sent 'for the perfecting of the saints, for the work of the ministry, for the edifying of the body of Christ', verse 12, so long as Christ reigns on high, and the saints exist below.

'Wherefore he saith', verse 8. Wherefore? But this word means 'On account of which, or, on which account.' That is, *on account of the preceding verse*, 'he saith'. Namely, *because of what had just been stated in verse 7, it follows*, 'When he ascended up on high, he led captivity captive, and gave gifts'–δοματα, *domata*–'unto men', Ephesians 4:8.

'Wherefore' following on *so as to elucidate verse 7, in which the gift of Christ was given to every one of 'us'*, the apostle explains the nature of the gift of Christ given unto every one of us, and none other, namely, the gift–or rather, the gifts–of the ascended Son of God from the excellent glory of heaven. Then, indubitably, the *domata*.

So the text reads; so the word *domata* demonstrates; so the context demands; and so both grammar and logic require in the conjunction of verses 7 and 8 beyond a peradventure. *Ergo*, verse 7 *must* refer to the *domata* and to the *domata* alone. *Quod erat demonstrandum*.

'Wherefore he saith, When he ascended up on high, he led captivity captive, and gave gifts unto men', Ephesians 4:8. This verse is a remarkable quotation from Psalm 68, which in itself speaks of entirely different events and occurrences in Israel, and, at that, in strange, mysterious, and apparently disconnected utterances, which, put together, make the psalm hard of interpretation.

From one such apparently random and arbitrary statement, abruptly the following words are uttered: 'Thou hast ascended on high, thou hast led captivity captive: thou hast received gifts for men; yea, for the rebellious also, that the LORD God might dwell among them', Psalm 68:18.

This is the verse quoted by Paul in Ephesians 4:8. It is the more remarkable that the psalmist does not appear to address– or even to be speaking of–Christ, and that even the events poetically portrayed concerning the history of Israel are at once disjointed and highly mystical in utterance throughout the context. Nevertheless, the apostle plucks out this verse and applies it to the ascension, further to his expounding the nature of the *domata*.

Without such an application by the apostle, it is impossible that anyone should have brought so obscure a verse to bear on the *domata*. However, by the inspiration of the Spirit, Paul not only does so, but moreover brings Ephesians 4:7 right into his exposition of the gifts of Christ *by this very quotation*, witness the introductory words, *'Wherefore he saith*,When he ascended up on high'; *then* follows the reference to Psalm 68:18.

Indeed, the psalms *do* speak of the ascension, albeit in a mystery. For example, 'The Lord said unto my Lord, Sit thou at my right hand, until I make thine enemies thy footstool', Psalm 110:1. This is quoted by Peter on the day of Pentecost, not now of the resurrection, of which David prophesied, and the apostles were witnesses, but of the ascension itself, in which the Son was exalted to the right hand of the Father, there to reign till his foes should be made his footstool, Acts 2:33-35.

Likewise the following Psalm: 'God is gone up with a shout, the Lord with the sound of a trumpet. Sing praises to God, sing praises: sing praises unto our King, sing praises. For God is the King of all the earth: sing ye praises with understanding. God reigneth over the heathen: God sitteth upon the throne of his holiness', Psalm 47:5-8.

Again, prophetically viewing Christ in the ascension the psalmist declares, 'For thou, Lord, art high above all the earth: thou art exalted far above all gods', Psalm 97:9. And this David echoes in Psalm 68:18, 'Thou hast ascended on high, thou hast led captivity captive.'

I do not intend to enlarge upon the mysteries of Psalm 68 as a whole, nor is this necessary. Suffice it to say with Peter that 'the prophets enquired and searched diligently, who prophesied of the grace that should come unto you: searching what, or what manner of time the Spirit of Christ which was in them did signify, when it testified beforehand the sufferings of Christ, and the glory that should follow.

'Unto whom it was revealed, that not unto themselves, but unto us they did minister the things, which are now reported unto you by them that have preached the gospel unto you with the Holy Ghost sent down from heaven; which things the angels desire to look into', I Peter 1:10-12. Of these things, Psalm 68:18, provides a choice example.

Because of the obvious difficulties in understanding the sequence of utterance in Psalm 68, whilst I have no intention of opening the psalm in its entirety, I will drop a few hints for the benefit of the reader concerning the context of verse 18.

The context is that of God arising and triumphing over his enemies on behalf of his people. He takes up the poor and despised, the captive outcasts of Israel in the distant lands of their bondage. He takes captivity captive. He calls his inheritance together. He leads them through the wilderness. He magnifies his glory at Sinai in the presence of all the people.

God arose, and his enemies were scattered. Pharaoh and his host perished in the Red sea. This victory, God's deliverances, made the earth to tremble, as he marched through the wilderness. The report thereof declared his goodness for the poor. This word was published by a great company. It was *God's* salvation.

From the land of their captivity, through the wilderness, God marched with his people, the land of their inheritance before their faces. The kings of Canaan fled apace. Zion was his choice. The mountains of Canaan trembled. The inhabitants of the land melted before the mighty power of God, his chariots, and his angels.

For his people got not the land in possession by their own sword, neither did their own arm save them: but thy right hand, and thine arm, and the light of thy countenance, because thou hadst a favour unto them. From the land of Egypt, Canaan was his objective, Zion his choice. This was the mountain of his inheritance.

As to the Canaanites, those who held the land in captivity, together with those whose stronghold was mount Zion, who held mount Zion captive, God scattered them all. The LORD arose to possess his holy mountain, he took mount Zion, that is, he ascended up on high, he led captivity captive. Here he chose to dwell. He would dwell among men, moreover giving gifts to the rebellious.

This made the earth to shake, the hills to leap. For the hill of God is as the hill of Bashan: an high hill as the hill of Bashan. Why leap ye, ye high hills? Zion is the hill which God desireth to dwell in; yea, the LORD will dwell in it for ever.

Thou hast ascended on high, thou hast led captivity captive: thou hast received gifts for men; yea, for the rebellious also, that the LORD God might dwell among them, Psalm 68:18.

But this ascent – as appears in Ephesians 4:8 – has a double meaning. That which was true in Israel was but a figure, a type, a shadow of good things to come, the substance of which should appear in the gospel of Christ. For, speaking through the first, initial, and outward circumstances, the Spirit declares of Christ in prophecy through the psalmist, speaking across the ages to the Son of God, '*Thou* hast ascended on high', Psalm 68:18.

'Wherefore he saith, When he ascended up on high, he led captivity captive, and gave gifts unto men', Ephesians 4:8. But this is not carnal: it is spiritual. It is not the earthly shadow: it is the heavenly reality.

Here is no mere ascent of a literal earthly mount in the land: here is the ascension into the heights of heaven by the victorious Son of God, in which he brings many sons to glory, whilst all his foes are made his footstool. This is called, 'leading captivity captive', and, in consequence, from the glory, 'giving gifts' – *domata* – 'unto men.'

However, the heights of the ascension can only be measured correctly from the point at which all commenced. This was not the grave. Much less was it from the earth after the resurrection. The point from which the Spirit measures the ascent of Christ is lower by far than both the earth and the grave.

This the apostle reveals in the following verses: 'Now that he ascended, what is it but that he also descended first into the lower parts of the earth? He that descended is the same also that ascended up far above all heavens, that he might fill all things', Ephesians 4:9,10.

Where the emphasis *first* is upon the *descent* of the Son of God. Because *that first* is the measure of the ascension. The height of his ascent is measured from the depth of his descent. And that descent is said to be 'into the lower parts of the earth', Ephesians 4:9.

In one sense the descent began from the deity and above all heavens. 'In the beginning was the Word, and the Word was with God, and the Word was God', John 1:1. 'And the Word was made flesh', John 1:14. Likewise, he 'being in the form of God, thought it not robbery to be equal with God: but made himself of no reputation, and took upon him the form of a servant, and was made in the likeness of men', Philippians 2:6,7.

These passages speak of the descent of the deity, in the person of the Son, at the incarnation. So that '*God* was manifest in the flesh', I Timothy 3:16. This declares the deity incarnate, and, if so, predicates a descent that staggers the imagination. Nevertheless, it is not the descent emphasised in Ephesians 4:9.

Ephesians 4:9 *presumes* both incarnation and crucifixion. But in fact the verse *commences* by stressing the depth of his descent *after burial. Then* he descended 'into the lower parts of the earth.' This brings one to the threshold of a vital part of the evangel that is virtually universally ignored, if not downright contradicted. But it is the evangel. It is the doctrine of Christ.

It *cannot* be ignored, much less contradicted, if one holds to the faith.

It is vital to perceive that Ephesians 4:9–and many other verses elsewhere–speak of what Christ did in the Spirit *whilst* his body lay dead in the tomb.

When the verse says 'he also descended first into the lower parts of the earth' it is impossible to suppose that this refers to his *body* being put in the sepulchre, which, in fact, was hewn out of rock *above the surface* of the earth, witness the stone rolled away from the mouth of the empty grave into which the first witnesses *walked*.

Besides, 'the lower parts of the earth' is synonymous with Revelation 5:3,13, where a distinction is made between 'in earth' or 'on earth' and 'under the earth', a metaphor for the underworld, just as is the expression 'the lower parts of the earth', Ephesians 4:9.

Moreover the depth of his descent 'into the lower parts of the earth', verse 9, is set in contrast with the height of his ascent 'far above all heavens', verse 10.

Where, if he has ascended up far above all that is visible or even imaginable over and above the heavens themselves, then it follows–since the descent and ascent are put in juxtaposition–that he first descended far below all that is visible or even imaginable beneath the depths of the earth or the burial places of the dead, namely, 'into the lower parts of the earth', or, the underworld.

David also speaks of a distinction *after* the death and burial of Christ, but *before* his resurrection, saying, 'Thou wilt not *leave* my *soul* in hell'–Hebrew, *sheol*, the underworld–'neither wilt thou suffer thine Holy One to *see* corruption'–that is, of the *body*, Psalm 16:10.

The apostle Peter, speaking by the Holy Ghost, interprets this prophecy on the day of Pentecost quoting David exactly, saying 'Thou wilt not leave my soul in hell, neither wilt thou suffer thine Holy One to see corruption', Acts 2:27.

Peter discerns this quotation from David, declaring that 'he seeing this before spake of the resurrection of Christ'–and, if so, of the period *after* his death but *before* his resurrection–'that his *soul* was not *left* in hell'–Greek, *hadēs*, the equivalent of *sheol*, the underworld–'neither his *flesh* did see corruption', Acts 2:30,31. This makes a clear distinction between the *soul* of Christ, after death, in respect of the underworld, and the *flesh* of Christ, after death, lying in the grave.

Paul confirms this truth in another way, asking a hypothetical question, as if in the place of those in doubt, 'Who shall descend into the deep? (that is, to bring up Christ again from the dead)', Romans 10:7. But Faith cries in triumph, There is no need; God hath raised him from the dead.

Nevertheless, to be valid, the rhetorical question *must assume the truth that after death Christ was in the deep.* If so, his *soul* descended into the deep. Now 'deep' here translates the Greek *abussos*, which answers to 'the abyss', another expression indicating the underworld. Then, into that, namely, 'the lower parts of the earth', or *sheol*, or else *hadēs*, his soul descended.

As to *what occurred* during the period between this descent of his soul, whilst his body lay dead in the sepulchre, and the time when he–that is, in his body–was raised from the dead by the glory of the Father, this is taught with perfect clarity in a passage so central to the evangel and to the mystery of the faith, that Paul states concerning this vital revelation: 'And without controversy great is the mystery of godliness', I Timothy 3:16.

The apostle continues, 'God was manifest in the flesh, justified in the Spirit, seen of angels, preached unto the Gentiles'–the Greek is *ethnos*, properly, Nations; that is, ethnic diversities–

'believed on in the world, received up into glory.' This completes the verse, I Timothy 3:16.

This verse utterly confounds both clergy and commentators, and, above all, wholly puzzles the theologians, not to mention equally self-conceited and know-all Brethren: but why? Element-ary, my dear reader. Why? *because they know nothing about the great mystery of godliness, being at once proud, dead, unspiritual, unex-perimental, and lost in the dark mists of their disobedient inventions in place of the divine and heavenly mystery of the faith once delivered to the saints.*

Hence, whilst to the simplest child it is obvious that I Timothy 3:16 consists of a series of six *consecutive* statements, because these supposedly mature know-alls cannot explain them in sequence, yet being too proud to confess their ignorance, they pretend – against even their own better judgment–that the statements are *random*, having no sequence at all! But if this is not God blinding their eyes, What is?

The verse commences, '*God was manifest in the flesh*'. This was the very first beginning of the descent, as has been demonstrated. The verse concludes, '*received up into glory*'. That was the utter-most end of the ascent, as has been clearly shown from the like contrast between descent and ascent in Ephesians 4:9,10.

Then how in heaven, on earth, or under the earth, can the four statements bracketed between his *descent* and his *ascent*, not on the one hand be *consequential*, and on the other, not refer to what happened in sequence between his descent and his ascent?

And, since these people think to evade the exposure of their incompetence by railing at me that I ought not to judge them–but it is Christ in me who judges them – in passing let me ask these haughty pretenders who *say* that they know what the verse means, Why no crucifixion? Why no death? Why no mention of the resurrection?

Come now: you know everything; I am nothing but a judge: then I invite you to show your knowledge, and confound my judgment. You say that you are of God, and that I cannot be, because I judge. Come now; if you are of God. Then tell us the meaning. But all we get from you is deafening silence: 'And the people answered him not a word', I Kings 18:21.

Of course they answered him not a word, any more than these answer me not a word, because God never put a word in their mouths, who go about as if they know everything; whereas he fills my mouth with his words, though of myself I know nothing.

This is the great mystery of *godliness*. Because *God* was manifested in the flesh. Every statement concerns the descent of the deity, and finally, the ascent into glory. If of the deity, even in such a context of being manifest in the flesh, one can never speak of death: only of what *God did*. He was manifested in the flesh, and, as to *that*, he was justified in the Spirit.

That is, *everything he came to achieve as becoming manifest in the flesh, had been achieved, and achieved with triumph*. He was wholly vindicated and justified in his having been made manifest in the flesh. But, first – mark that, *first* – that justification was *in the Spirit*. Not in the flesh in which he had been manifest from the first.

Nevertheless, because he *was* justified, this means that he had *finished the work which he came to do*. The Spirit justified this, and verified it by a sevenfold witness, *immediately victory had been won*. Now, as to the flesh, that means *after the cross, and following the burial*.

But these statements concern *God*; they concern *the deity*. Then, not the flesh in which he was manifested, but he who was manifested in that flesh, is now traced from descent to ascent, in all that is most critical of his divine pathway. At this point, *everything accomplished for ever*, immediately, but *immediately*, he was justified in the Spirit.

Then – and not till then – *then* he was 'seen of angels'. So that this could not refer to those angels who had seen him at and following the incarnation, or during the period of his being manifest in 'the days of his flesh'. This must refer to those angels *who had not seen him thus*, who, following the justification of all his work on earth, *in the Spirit saw him now*.

Why? I will tell you why. Because having wrought everlasting victory to perfection, justified in the Spirit, in that same Spirit *he went down and proclaimed the same to these spirits here called angels*. Proclaimed, yes; and no more. *They* were left in everlasting chains, under darkness, unto the judgment of the great day. These were the angels that sinned, II Peter 2:4.

Next, *after* this – for the angels, being greater in power and might, were to see – and hear the proclamation – first. These were the angels that sinned, and caused to sin, in the days of Noah. But the sinning nations, carried away in the flood with the destruction of the old world, came next in order.

To these the tremendous voice of Almighty God echoed and re-echoed in the depths of the underworld as it proclaimed – the Greek is *kērussō*, to proclaim; to announce; or to herald – the vindication of Noah, and of the election of God, *seen* in his having been justified in the Spirit. And, by the Spirit, he made the proclamation.

What a justification this was! How great, you shall know when you behold with your eyes the whole of time from the beginning unfold – and, as it were, unreel – before your astounded vision in the last, the great day of judgment.

As to the souls of those wicked nations which perished in the flood, called the old world, following this proclamation, their doom sealed, these await with anguish and trembling the resurrection of the unjust, and the sentence of everlasting punishment in the great day of God. *They* know it: do *you* know it?

Immediately following, the ascent begins. First, from angels and men in the underworld, to whom had been thundered out the tremendous vindication of God from the beginning of time up to the overwhelming victory of the cross. A victory achieved, that is, *before* the descent. And now, from the deep ascending up to the face of the earth, he is *'believed on in the world'.*

God, who was manifested in the flesh, justified in the Spirit, seen of angels, proclaimed unto the nations, is now 'believed on in the world'. That is, he is risen. Then what can they say who are his, but, falling on their face, cry out 'My Lord *and my* God', John 20:28. Now, *these* believed on him in the world.

So the eyewitnesses affirmed, saying, 'That which was from the beginning, which we have heard, which we have seen with our eyes, which we have looked upon, and our hands have handled, of the Word of life; for the *life was manifested*, and we have seen it, and bear witness, and show unto you *that eternal life'*, I John 1:1,2.

What is this but that God was manifested in the flesh, justified in the Spirit, seen of angels, proclaimed unto the nations, and now—*as God*—believed on in the world. But God in three persons:

'We have *seen*, and show unto you *that eternal life*, which *was* with the Father'—before being manifest in the flesh—'and was manifested unto *us.*' Supremely manifested, that is, as victorious over all, when, on earth, risen from the dead, one with the Father and with the Spirit, he was seen for forty days. If so, 'believed on in the world'.

First by the eyewitnesses: 'Him God raised up the third day, and showed him openly; not to all the people, but unto witnesses chosen before of God, even to us, who did eat and drink with him after he rose from the dead', Acts 10:40,41. This is to be 'believed on in the world', that is, following his prior descent into the lower parts of the earth, yet before his being received up into glory.

'He rose again the third day according to the scriptures: and that he was seen of Cephas, then of the twelve: after that, he was seen of above five hundred brethren at once; of whom the greater part remain unto this present, but some are fallen asleep. After that, he was seen of James; then of all the apostles. And last of all he was seen of me also', I Corinthians 15:4-8. This is to be 'believed on in the world'.

'Until the day in which he was taken up, after that he through the Holy Ghost had given commandments unto the apostles whom he had chosen: to whom also he showed himself alive after his passion by many infallible proofs, being seen of them forty days', Acts 1:2,3. This is to be 'believed on in the world'.

Finally—yet not finally to perfection: finally in the great mystery of godliness revealed in six consequential statements in I Timothy 3:16–'received up into glory.' This is the height of the ascension, of which we cannot now speak particularly, since we have yet somewhat to add to the opening of the words, 'he also descended first into the lower parts of the earth', Ephesians 4:9.

The apostle Peter enlarges upon this essential evangelical truth of the great mystery of godliness, when, consonant with 'seen of angels' in I Timothy 3:16, he declares, 'God spared not the angels that sinned, but cast them down to'—it is not 'hell' at all; neither is it *hadēs*, nor yet the abyss: it is *tartarus*, the deepest depths–'delivered into chains of darkness, to be reserved unto judgment', II Peter 2:4.

Of these Peter wrote earlier, saying that Christ was 'put to death in the flesh, but quickened by the Spirit: by which also he went and'–it is not 'preached': it is *kērussō*, as in I Timothy 3:16 – 'proclaimed unto the spirits'–not *souls* notice: *spirits*; that is, the angels that sinned.

For 'he maketh his angels spirits', Hebrews 1:7. Then, though fallen angels, still *spirits* – 'in prison; which sometime were disobedient, when once the longsuffering of God waited in the days of Noah', I Peter 3:19,20. This verifies the truth opened in I Timothy 3:16.

The book of Jude also confirms the truth of the fallen angels being confined in the deepest depths: 'And the angels which kept not their first estate, but left their own habitation, he hath reserved in everlasting chains under darkness unto the judgment of the great day', Jude 6.

To these, even though they were in the deepest depths, the proclamation reached, heralding the glorious triumph of God over all the age, every enemy, and, here in particular, over all the consequences of the disobedience of the angels whose sin brought about the judgment of the old world.

To such depths–the deepest depths–the proclamation of the victory–reaching throughout all ages and over all time–was sounded forth by him who descended into the lower parts of the earth.

The apostle Peter goes even further than the scope of I Timothy 3:16 in the following scripture: 'For this cause *was the gospel preached*'–this is *not* '*kērussō*', to make proclamation; it is *euaggelizomai, to preach the evangel* – 'also to them that are dead, that they might be judged according to men in the flesh, but live according to God in the spirit', I Peter 4:6.

Who were those dead whose life when in the flesh was judged? Who preached the gospel unto them? When did this take place? And what was the effect?

47

Those dead whose life in the flesh was judged were the old testament saints. The end of these, after death, was utterly different from that of sinners. Nevertheless, the souls of both went to the underworld, but their existence *there* was entirely separate. The saints were those 'carried by angels' into 'Abraham's bosom'. Sinners were those separated into a place of torment.

'And it came to pass, that the beggar died, and was carried by the angels into Abraham's bosom: the rich man also died, and was buried; and in *hadēs*'—it should not be 'hell': it is *hadēs*—'he lift up his eyes, being in torments, and seeth Abraham afar off, and Lazarus in his bosom', Luke 16:22,23. Then, they were not *so* far apart as not to be visible to each other.

Nor were they so distant that they could not communicate: 'But Abraham said, Son, remember that thou in thy lifetime receivedst thy good things, and likewise Lazarus evil things: but now he is comforted, and thou art tormented.

'And beside all this, between us and you there is a great gulf fixed: so that they which would pass from hence to you cannot; neither can they pass to us, that would come from thence', Luke 16:26. No doubt in this parable Jesus used metaphor. But what of that? It is metaphor used by the Lord to convey *the truth*.

That truth denoted the souls of men whose bodies had died being strictly divided into that seed reckoned as children of Abraham by faith, and those faithless sinners who were not counted for the seed. These were separated by 'a great gulf' but, in the parable, it was possible to communicate, at least by vision and speech, from one side to the other.

Hence the one *sheol*, or underworld, was divided on the one hand to the blessing of Abraham's bosom, and, across the impassable gulf, on the other hand to the torment of the curse. After death the souls of all the dead were irrevocably committed to the one or other.

That is, until God was manifested in the flesh, and justified in the Spirit. Namely, until Christ through death destroyed him that had the power of death, that is, the devil, and delivered them who through fear of death were all their lifetime subject to bondage, Hebrews 2:14,15.

That is, until Messiah finished the transgression, made an end of sins, made reconciliation for iniquity, and brought in everlasting righteousness, Daniel 9:24. Namely, until in death Christ accomplished redemption for all that by faith had looked for salvation from the coming Messiah since the beginning of the world until the cross, and for all that should ever believe on him after the cross till the end of the world.

That is, until in the fulness of his glorious accomplished victory, Christ descended in the Spirit to proclaim to the angelic spirits in prison and to the tormented souls of the nations in *hadēs* the triumph in which they had neither believed from prophecy, nor obeyed with foresight. For he 'was seen of angels, proclaimed unto the nations', when he 'descended into the lower parts of the earth.'

That is, until in his descent by the Spirit he 'preached the gospel to them that are dead' from righteous Abel to believing Noah, thence to every one who had died in the faith which Abraham had yet being uncircumcised, all resting in Abraham's bosom, till the mighty conqueror who had accomplished their redemption at last, preached the same in his descent thereafter.

This which he had just accomplished was that which they had believed would be fulfilled when he came. Thus he was the Lamb slain from the foundation of the world, believed upon by all who died in faith, looking to him and for him who should justify them by his blood at his coming. This he had done. And that he preaches to their believing souls.

This is called his 'preaching the gospel to them that are dead'. Though in Abraham's bosom, yet still both Abraham and all the great multitude of believing souls yearned for the fulfilment of all that in which they had trusted, for which they died in faith.

In their lifetime it had been evident that they were the righteous, or the just, for, 'the just shall live by faith'.

And now their faith was justified, for when Christ preached the gospel to these that were dead, behold, their lifetime – being judged according to the life of faith which they had lived in the days of their flesh – itself declared their belief and trust in the coming Messiah.

Thus they were judged according to men in the flesh, for that which they had believed afar off when they were alive in the world, was what they heard in the Spirit by the gospel now being preached unto them. That very gospel, yea, that same Jesus, albeit seen and heard dimly in their lifetime, was what they saw and heard so clearly in the gospel presently being preached unto them by their descended Redeemer.

That was what, and *he* was whom, they had believed in the days of their pilgrimage, and now, their redemption having been fully accomplished, their justification already having been wrought, they were in spirit to ascend with him to heavenly glory, 'the spirits of just men made perfect', Hebrews 12:23.

'The spirits of just men made perfect'? To whom else *can* this refer but to the old testament saints, and *all* the old testament saints, namely *every one* of those just men? 'Made perfect'? Yes, since the time that Christ preached the gospel to their awaiting souls in Abraham's bosom, carrying their – relative – captivity captive as he led them up to the perfection of heavenly glory.

That 'we are come' unto these, Hebrews 12:22, who are ourselves justified under the new testament, shows that – there being none other just men than these – these are the just who had died in faith under the old testament. They await us; we are come unto them; or, we are yet coming unto them.

Where are they now? Not in Abraham's bosom in the underworld as was once the case before Christ descended, but now in glory, for they first, then we, are 'come unto mount Sion, and unto the city of the living God, the *heavenly* Jerusalem, and to an innumerable company of'–holy–'*angels*'.

We are come 'to the general assembly and church of the firstborn, which are written *in heaven, and to God the Judge of all, and to the spirits of just men made perfect, and to Jesus* the mediator of *the new covenant*'–that stands in everlasting heavenly glory– 'and to the blood of sprinkling'–namely, *on the propitiatory before the Majesty on high*, Hebrews 12:22-24.

Of this victory of the cross, a certain witness–among others– was borne immediately: 'Jesus, when he had cried again with a loud voice, yielded up the ghost. And, behold, the veil of the temple was rent in twain from the top to the bottom; and the earth did quake, and the rocks rent.'

'*And the graves were opened; and many bodies of the saints which slept arose*, and came out of the graves *after* his resurrection, and went into the holy city, and appeared unto many', Matthew 27:50-53. Here is a witness indeed. The souls of *all* were delivered. But the bodies of *some* were a sign.

The Lord's ascent in victory, triumphing over all by the cross, bringing to glory every single saint who had ever believed upon him, all the just who had lived by faith, and who had died in faith, whose souls had patiently waited in Abraham's bosom: What is this? It is called 'leading captivity captive', Ephesians 4:8.

As to the glorious heavenly height to which the whole of this erstwhile captivity was led, this is the inheritance, Colossians 1:12, of those who now 'live according to God in the spirit', I Peter 4:6.

This Christ achieved by his death for all the old testament saints *after* he descended, and *when* he had ascended: 'Wherefore he saith, When he ascended up on high, he led captivity captive, and gave gifts unto men.'

'Now that he *ascended*'–leading so great a multitude of once captive souls, who had awaited his redemption by faith–'what is it but that *he also descended first*'–descended first? But descended where?–'into the lower parts of the earth', Ephesians 4:8,9.

Hence it is that when *we* die after the flesh, our souls immediately ascend to be with the Lord. Thus John in vision sees all the elect–signified by the twelve patriarchs and the twelve apostles–in the twenty-four elders on thrones about the throne of God and of the Lamb.

Whence it follows that–unlike the old testament saints who waited–we who are in and of the new testament, falling asleep, are carried in our souls immediately into the heavenly glory, thence to 'be ever with the Lord'.

'He that descended is the same also that ascended up far above all heavens, that he might fill all things', Ephesians 4:10. Here two things immediately impress the reader. First, *this was a verified, witnessed, attested historical event*. It happened, and it was seen to have happened.

Second, over and above the basic *fact* of the historical event, what was *not* seen by the eyewitnesses was *the height to which the ascension reached*. It passed from view when the eye could see no more. Then, it entered into dimensions beyond human capacity to comprehend. It passed all understanding, because it lay beyond man's faculties to grasp.

But faith believes and grasps the doctrine that sets forth the ascension, fully acknowledging that the bodily ascent of Christ 'above all heavens' lies utterly beyond man's natural ability even to imagine. Then don't imagine it.

Simply receive the truth and believe it. And know this: you will surely find it so in the end, at the coming again – and descent – of Christ. Blessed are they that have not seen, and yet have believed, John 20:29. This refers to the resurrection of his body. Then how much more of his ascension?

And so Peter tells you: 'Whom having not seen, ye love; in whom, though now ye see him not, yet believing, ye rejoice with joy unspeakable and full of glory: receiving the end of your faith, even the salvation of your souls', I Peter 1:8,9.

Thus Paul cautions us against the carnal mind and natural intellect, assuring us that his apostolic warfare was against such things, 'Casting down imaginations, and every high thing that exalteth itself against the knowledge of God, and bringing into captivity every thought to the obedience of Christ', II Corinthians 10:5.

Wherefore? Because nothing is more destructive of faith than human reasoning. Which is not surprising, since 'To be carnally minded is death.' Worse: it is death unnaturally animated by implacable hostility: 'because the carnal mind is enmity against God', Romans 8:7. Why? Because it is fallen. It is earthly, sensual, and devilish, James 3:15. It cannot believe, it will not believe, and it is enmity against belief: 'For whatsoever is not of faith is sin', Romans 14:23.

Then it is by faith that, believing ourselves risen again with Christ, we 'seek those things which are above, where Christ sitteth on the right hand of God.' Indeed, dead to reasonings, imaginings, worldly and unbelieving thoughts, the just live by faith: 'for ye are dead, and your life is hid with Christ in God', Colossians 3:1-3. This is to answer by faith to the revelation of the height of the ascension.

Mark tells of the eyewitnesses of the ascension: 'So then after the Lord had spoken unto them, he was received up into heaven,

and sat on the right hand of God. And they'–the eleven–
'went forth, and preached everywhere, the Lord working with
them, and confirming the word with signs following. Amen',
Mark 16:19,20.

John however records the words of Jesus himself to Mary
Magdalene, after he was risen from the dead: the Lord declares
the triumph of his death for his own–calling them 'my brethren'–
even though he had not yet ascended to his Father. But he
sends her with this message: 'Go to my brethren, and say unto
them, I ascend unto my Father, and your Father; and to my
God, and your God', John 20:17. This testifies to the height and
to the glory of the ascension.

Luke bears record precisely of that which was seen by the
eleven: 'And he led them out as far as to Bethany, and he lifted
up his hands, and blessed them. And it came to pass, while he
blessed them, he was parted from them, and carried up into
heaven', Luke 24:50,51. So that their last view of him, as he
ascended, was that of his nail-pierced hands lifted up together
with his voice, blessing them indeed. And so it is to this day.

For their word was blessed to multitudes and generations,
whether spoken or written, as he saith, 'But ye shall receive
power, after that the Holy Ghost is come upon you: and ye'–
the eleven–'shall be witnesses unto me both in Jerusalem, and
in all Judea, and in Samaria, and unto the uttermost part of
the earth.

'And when he had spoken these things, *while they beheld*, he
was taken up; and a cloud received him out of their sight. And
while they looked steadfastly toward heaven as he went up,
behold, two men stood by them in white apparel;

'Which also said, Ye men of Galilee, why stand ye gazing up
into heaven? this same Jesus, which is taken up from you into
heaven, shall so come in like manner as ye have seen him go
into heaven', Acts 1:8-11.

When the Holy Ghost had been shed forth on the day of Pentecost, Peter, standing up with the eleven, bore witness first to the resurrection of Christ, then to his ascension, calling David to record: 'For David speaketh concerning him, I foresaw the Lord always before my face, for he is on my right hand, that I should not be moved:

'Therefore did my heart rejoice, and my tongue was glad; moreover also my flesh shall rest in hope: Because thou wilt not leave my soul in *hadēs*, neither wilt thou suffer thine Holy One to see corruption. Thou hast made known to me the ways of life; thou shalt make me full of joy with thy countenance.

'Men and brethren, let me freely speak unto you of the patriarch David, that he is both dead and buried, and his sepulchre is with us unto this day. Therefore being a prophet, and knowing that God had sworn with an oath to him, that of the fruit of his loins, according to the flesh, he would raise up Christ to sit on his throne;

'He seeing this before spake of the resurrection of Christ, that *his* soul was not left in *hadēs*, neither *his* flesh did see corruption. This Jesus hath God raised up, whereof we all are witnesses', Acts 2:25-32. This is both the prophecy and the *eyewitness account* of the resurrection of Jesus, 'Whom God hath raised up, having loosed the pains of death: because it was not possible that he should be holden of it', Acts 2:24.

The testimony to Christ's ascension – forty days after his resurrection – now follows: 'Therefore *being by the right hand of God exalted*, and having received of the Father the promise of the Holy Ghost, *he* hath shed forth this, which *ye* now see and hear.

'For *David* is not ascended into the heavens: but he saith himself, The LORD said unto *my* Lord, Sit *thou* on my right hand, until I make thy foes thy footstool. Therefore'– continues Peter – 'let all the house of Israel know assuredly, that God hath made *that same Jesus*, whom ye have crucified, both Lord and Christ', Acts 2:33-36.

This concludes the *eyewitness*–as well as the *prophetic*–testimony to the *ascension* of the *risen* Lord.

David had uttered and written the prophecy which Peter quotes on the day of Pentecost *some one thousand years before*. Now, How can anyone reasonably doubt the resurrection and ascension, seeing such things were both spoken and recorded in close detail *even before the millennium preceding that in which these things took place?* And this is not to mention the *eyewitness* in the event.

How could this be, had not God revealed the future so long before on the one hand, and set aside all natural laws, bringing to light dimensions undreamed of and staggering all reason on the other hand? Yet, doing both so as *indisputable facts* irrefutably supported the supernatural mysteries *in both cases*.

If any desire a proof of the infallible inspiration of holy scripture, this provides it: just as much because of what was *foreseen in detail* a thousand years before it happened, as in the case that the same thing was *witnessed by impeccable eyewitnesses*–plural–a thousand years later. Then, beyond any shadow of doubt, let all men be advertised *that the ascension really took place, and that Christ really is on the right hand of God at this moment.*

Let no one overlook the truth that it is the factual evidence to the ascension of Christ that is presented in holy writ. Nothing less than *facts*, concerning first David, then the eleven, appear before the reader, in the light of time and eternity, of things first foreseen, then visibly outworked, next witnessed and verified, and finally passed into the heavens.

Thereafter, all being invisible, outside of human comprehension, and pertaining to dimensions beyond all faculties and senses to realize, it is a matter of what was revealed by inspiration of the Holy Ghost to the chosen apostles in the doctrine of Christ, and recorded in the epistles of the new testament.

What is revealed concerning the work of Christ in the ascension may differ from one epistle to another. For example, in Ephesians it is a question of Headship. In Hebrews, however, it is a matter of Priesthood. But since the present state of the enquiry concerns the ascension as such, whilst Headship is the ultimate question, the revelation from Hebrews regarding Priesthood is of no mean weight to establish the doctrine.

Consider: Concerning the Son it is revealed – revealed, mind: all this doctrine is spiritually *revealed* by the Holy Ghost *after* the Son had passed from the sight of the apostles into the heavens – 'When he had by himself purged our sins, *sat down on the right hand of the Majesty on high*', Hebrews 1:3.

Again: 'To which of the angels said he at any time, *Sit on my right hand, until I make thine enemies thy footstool?*', Hebrews 1:13. Or consider this: 'Thou crownedst him with glory and honour, and didst set him *over* the works of thy hands: Thou hast put all things *under his feet*', Hebrews 2:7,8.

Once more: 'Seeing then that we have a great high priest, *that is passed into the heavens*, Jesus the Son of God', Hebrews 4:14.

Likewise, 'Christ glorified not himself to be made an high priest; but he that said unto him, Thou art my Son, today have I begotten thee'–that is in the resurrection from the dead, Acts 13:33–'As he saith also in another place'– concerning the ascension, and following the resurrection, Acts 2:34, Psalm 110:1,2, and 4–'Thou art a priest for ever after the order of Melchisedec', Hebrews 5:5,6.

See now what *revelation* flows down from the glory: 'For such an high priest became us, who is holy, harmless, undefiled, separate from sinners, *and made higher than the heavens*', Hebrews 7:26. 'We have such an high priest, *who is set on the right hand of the throne of the Majesty in the heavens*', Hebrews 8:1.

'For if he were on earth'—even though risen from the dead, as he was those forty days—'he should not be a priest, seeing that there are priests that offer gifts according to the law', Hebrews 8:4; 'But now hath he obtained *a more excellent ministry*'—that is, above all heavens, according to the evangel—Hebrews 8:6.

'But Christ being come an high priest of good things to come, by a greater and more perfect tabernacle, not made with hands, that is to say, not of this building; neither by the blood of goats and calves, *but by his own blood he entered in once into the holy place, having obtained eternal redemption for us*', Hebrews 9:11,12.

'For Christ is not entered into the holy places made with hands, which are the figures of the true; *but into heaven itself*, now to appear *in the presence of God* for us', Hebrews 9:24.

And let the weight of the following passage, delivered by inspiration of the Holy Ghost, concerning things unseen, sink down into the ears of him that hath ears to hear: 'But this man, after he had offered one sacrifice for sins for ever, *sat down on the right hand of God; from henceforth expecting till his enemies be made his footstool*', Hebrews 10:12,13.

Or this: 'Having therefore, brethren, boldness to enter into *the holiest* by the blood of Jesus, by a new and living way, which he hath consecrated for us, *through the veil, that is to say, his flesh*; and having *an high priest over the house of God*; let us *draw near* with a true *heart* in full assurance of faith', Hebrews 10:19-22.

How greatly, therefore, does the ascension inspire us to keep 'Looking unto Jesus the author and finisher of our faith; who for the joy that was set before him endured the cross, despising the shame, *and is set down at the right hand of the throne of God*', Hebrews 12:2.

Nevertheless it is not his ascension in order to occupy the office of Priesthood, as in Hebrews, but rather his ascending to fulfil the position of *Headship* that concerns the epistle to the

Ephesians. And if of *Headship*, then to make manifest the mystery of the *Body*. And if of the *Body*, then of the heavenly gifts essential to bring in this same fellowship of the mystery.

Hence Paul stresses the exaltation of Christ even from so great a glory as that of his resurrection from the dead: 'and set him at his own right hand in the heavenly places, far above all principality, and power, and might, and dominion, and every name that is named, not only in this world, but also in that which is to come.'

Indeed, from such an ultimate descent, to such an absolute ascent, how can this his sovereign majesty over all be surprising? 'And hath put all things under his feet, and gave him to be the head over all things to the *ecclesia*, which is *his body*, the *fulness of him* that filleth all in all', Ephesians 1:20-23.

'Whereof', declares Paul, 'I was made a minister.' How was this? 'How that by revelation he made known unto me the mystery.' The mystery? Yes, of the unsearchable riches of Christ, 'to make all'– saints–'see what is the fellowship of the mystery', Ephesians 3:3,7-9.

Whereof he was made a minister? Oh? Who made him a minister? Evidently, Christ, from the excellent glory. For from thence came the voice from heaven, 'For I have appeared unto thee for this purpose, to make thee a minister', Acts 26:16.

How should Christ from above the heaven of heavens do this? He should do it by his divine and heavenly initiative in calling Paul to the office of minister, a unique *doma*, the gift of Christ from heaven.

'Whereof I was made a minister, according to the gift'– that is *dōrea*, a word closely related to *doma*– 'the gift of the grace of God given unto me by the effectual working of his power', Ephesians 3:7. That was how it was done. That was how he was made a minister. *And I tell you of a truth, for all man's invented substitutes, there is no other way into the ministry, just as there can be no other 'ministers' entitled to the name.*

How *could* there be any other ministers, or any other way, when *the Son of God from heaven* sends the ministers he calls *domata*, and when the *effectual working of God's power* gives them–*dōrea*–the ability? Where is man in that? Where is the 'church' in that? Where are 'divinity schools' in that? There is *nothing* of any such things in that. The real thing is *all of God*.

By this means, Christ having ascended, the Holy Ghost having descended, the saints are brought into the fulness, and into the knowledge of the fulness. 'And hath put all things under his feet, and gave him to be the head over all things to the *ecclesia*, which is his body, the fulness of him that filleth all in all', Ephesians 1:22,23.

But first, he descended. 'He that descended is the same also that ascended up far above all heavens, *that he might fill all things*', Ephesians 4:10. Nothing in the deepest abyss below, nothing in the glory far above all heavens, but that he took it all in, and *that* in person, putting all things in their place relative to his victory, his authority, and his proclamation, 'that he might fill all things'.

Further to which–to affirm which–by the Holy Ghost from heaven, by the effectual working of God's power, by his sole sovereign initiative and authority, from far above all heavens *he ordained and does ordain every single one of the ministers whom he sends.*

'And he gave'–Ephesians 3:8; 4:7,8,11; *here is the root of the word domata*–'he gave some, apostles; and some, prophets; and some, evangelists; and some, pastors and teachers', Ephesians 4:11.

In a word *he gave* his own chosen, called, prepared, ordained, and sent *ministers; he gave their persons;* some to be this, some to be that, some to be the other, but all *given alike*–in a mystery–*from the ascension, far above all heavens,* and all as one called by the common name given to the ministers of Christ from the glory, namely, the *domata,* Ephesians 4:8,11.

It is of this that the apostle Paul speaks precisely when he declares, 'And God hath set some in the *ecclesia,* first apostles, secondarily prophets, thirdly teachers', I Corinthians 12:28.

In order to show the distinction between these heavenly gifts of Christ from his ascended glory, as opposed to the gifts of the Spirit descended to glorify Christ in the body on earth, the preceding doctrine has been opened.

So that the first, second, and third gifts mentioned in I Corinthians 12:28, respectively, indicate the *doma,* each in his proper rank, yet, as a whole, all having those distinctive features unique to the *domata.*

Whereas First Corinthians does not reveal the position of the *ecclesia* in relation to Christ in the ascension–but rather in terms of the Spirit during the time of pilgrimage on earth–Ephesians does: and hence it is from this epistle that the brief mention of the *domata* in I Corinthians 12:28 has been elucidated.

'After that'–continues the apostle–'after that miracles'–that is, works of power–'then gifts'–*charismata*–'of healings, helps, governments, diversities of tongues', I Corinthians 12:28.

The most obvious distinction between 'apostles, prophets, teachers', and *after that* 'miracles, gifts of healings, helps, governments, diversities of tongues', I Corinthians 12:28, lies in the fact that the former–the *domata*–are *persons,* whereas the latter–the *charismata*–are not: they are *gifts given to persons.*

And yet in one sense–despite the disparity–there is a relation between the two. Indeed, the very words 'after that' seem to imply a certain potential inter-relationship between the *domata* and the *charismata*. And this is reinforced by the apostle with the words concerning the *charismata*, 'covet earnestly the *best gifts*', I Corinthians 12:31, in which brethren are encouraged to reach out to the highest in order that they might edify the most.

Coveting earnestly the best gifts may well lead to the Lord taking up in a far wider, heavenly, and divine way those whose excellence appeared in their charismatic ministry in the body of Christ where it had pleased God at the first to set them.

Timothy provides the perfect example of this. During Paul's first great apostolic circuit, he preached and taught the evangel for some time at Iconium, then Lystra, and also Derbe. On his return he confirmed the disciples in each city, exhorting them to continue in the faith, ordaining elders in each *ecclesia* with prayer and fasting.

Then, the brethren would have been graven upon his heart, and he would have observed the operation of God, the work of the Lord, and the ministration of the Spirit in each of the three congregations. If so, he would have rejoiced in the faith and background of Timothy, his mother Eunice, and his grandmother Lois. This young man was already marked out.

After a very considerable passage of time Paul returned, and, not to his surprise, found that in the interval Timothy 'was well reported of by the brethren', not only in the *ecclesia* in which he met, but likewise in the two congregations gathered in the adjoining cities. Here the brethren gave evidence of Timothy's 'making full proof of thy ministry'.

From that time forth Paul took him to be with him in his apostolic labours. This had been confirmed by prophecy–whether in the *ecclesia* at Iconium, Lystra, or Derbe–and by the laying on of Paul's hands, with the laying on of the hands of the presbytery. From then on a new field opened up to the young man whom Paul calls 'my dearly beloved son'.

But what was Timothy's ministry in terms of gift? First, in his own city, then, increasing, in the two adjoining assemblies, it was that of the exercise of his gift from the Spirit, nor was this ever to depart from him: it was but to increase in him.

Wherefore Paul exhorts, 'Neglect not the gift'–*charismatos*–'that is in thee', I Timothy 4:14. And again, 'Stir up the gift'–*charisma*–'of God, which is in thee', II Timothy 1:6. If so, Timothy began with the gift of the Spirit bestowed upon him in the body. In this he abounded and increased in his love for the brethren. And for this cause Paul took him to be with him.

How could one deny that as Paul's 'own son in the faith', with whom Paul associated himself in addressing the epistles to the *ecclesia*, Timothy, who was 'my workfellow', and 'fellowlabourer in the evangel of Christ', commanded to ordain overseers, servants, and elders, receiving the charge in the absence of the apostle, I say, Who could deny that after such faithful diligence, the gift–*doma*–of Christ did not rest upon 'brother Timothy'?

This progression, this elevation, this taking up the choice gifts, coupled with earnest zeal, of the Spirit and by the Lord, appears to the encouragement of all whose motive is nothing other than love. For this cause alone such 'covet earnestly the best gifts'. Thus, for example, prophecy, first a gift of the Spirit, transcends to become 'prophet', distinctly a gift from Christ.

Wherefore all are drawn in their measure to increase by the magnanimity of the Spirit, and by the gift of the grace of Christ, that love should find its fullest expression, unhindered and unlimited, from charity out of a pure heart, and a good conscience, and of faith unfeigned.

No wonder then, that Timothy is to 'do the work of an evangelist', II Timothy 4:5, a gift proper to the *domata*, Ephesians 4:11. Nothing but encouragement for faith; nothing but enlargement for love; and nothing but fulfilment in the 'perfecting of the saints, the work of the ministry, the edifying of the body of Christ', Ephesians 4:12.

Then, 'according as God hath dealt to every man the measure of faith', the saints are exhorted to increase in all humility and lowliness, each preferring the other in love, but every one encouraging the other to go on to perfection in fulness, for, 'Whosoever will, let him take the water of life freely'.

With the ascension of the Son above all heavens to the right hand of the Majesty on high, presenting the full accomplishment of his redemptive work, effectual from the beginning of the world till the last day of its dissolution, he received of the Father the promise of the Holy Ghost, which he shed forth abundantly on the day of Pentecost.

This brought in the body of Christ. In the light of the First Epistle to the Corinthians, the body is viewed as constituted by the Holy Ghost dwelling within the saints united in the faith in their pilgrimage here below. This position, however, is not that envisaged in Ephesians, where the body of Christ is seen as one with the Head in the heavenlies, and dead with Christ to all below. First Corinthians hardly views the saints in connection with the ascension as such: all the focus is upon the body on earth.

The analogy of this appeared in the tabernacle in the wilderness, in which the presence of God abode in the midst of Israel from just after their deliverance from Egypt until their entrance into the promised land. This was the testimony throughout their pilgrimage. In a figure, it was let down from heaven.

The tent of witness had no fixed abode on earth: it was moveable: it had no floor. The presence of God was passing through the wilderness with the pilgrim people of God, till they ascended into the promised land. Just so 'the testimony of Christ was confirmed in you', I Corinthians 1:6.

Had they fallen? Yes, but, 'God is faithful', I Corinthians 1:9, and the apostle labours for them in prayer and by letter. All things having been set in order on earth, therefore, according to the word of God and the nature of the testimony, finally the pilgrim *ecclesia* is caught up to the glory of heaven in I Corinthians 15.

This is the glory that shines before the face – yea, and in the heart– of all those travelling in unity through the wilderness of this present world as pilgrims and strangers with their pathway set onwards toward Zion. It is this inshining glory that illuminates the body of Christ on earth.

Nevertheless God makes full provision for this pilgrimage of the *ecclesia*, the body of Christ, filled with the Holy Ghost on earth. For 'God hath set some in the *ecclesia*, first apostles, secondarily prophets, thirdly teachers, *after that* works of power, *charismata* of healings, helps, governments, diversities of tongues', I Corinthians 12:28.

Following on from the three classes of *persons* whom God hath set in the *ecclesia*, first apostles, secondarily prophets, thirdly teachers – though not here expressly so-called, yet still *domata*– the apostle proceeds to denominate certain *charismata*. These, of course, are not persons, but *gifts*, given to members of the body of Christ.

Five such *charismata* are mentioned, three of which had been named before in the hypothetical list in I Corinthians 12:8-10. But two had not. Nor were these two – quite apart from the *domata* – immaterial to the Corinthians. They were *essential*. Yet they were conspicuous by their absence.

When one considers the division, the fornication, one brother taking another to law, the incest, the riotous assembly, the abuse of the supper, the neglect of warnings, the eating and drinking not only what had been offered to idols, but consumed at table within the temples of those idols, the abuse of the sign of tongues, the disorderly behaviour of women, the allowance of division and disorder, disbelief in the resurrection, and I know not what else; I ask, Who was 'helpful'?

Those of the house of Chloe were 'helpful', I Corinthians 1:11. They which were approved by standing fast in the one unity despite the divisions all around them were 'helpful', I Corinthians 11:19. Above all, Paul was 'helpful', and, standing with him, brother Sosthenes, I Corinthians 1:1. All these were helpful.

Yes, but where was the *gift of the Spirit*, most surely needed in plurality in the unhelpful chaos at Corinth, namely, the gift of 'helps', I Corinthians 12:28?

Who desired *that* gift? It was non-existent. Indeed, it was despised. But the Corinthians *needed* help–in the spiritual gift of it; *and* as multiplied–more than they dreamed of: yet help was the last thing the various opinions and divisions thought that they required. To them, *others* needed it: and *they* shouted it. But the truth was, they *all* needed 'helps' from the Spirit.

Equally–if not more–was it so with 'governments'. The riotous meetings, the carnal divisions, the absence of control, the breakdown of authority, the erroneous factions, the ap-palling misbehaviour, all this gave rise to the conclusion that they were ungovernable. And so did the total absence of any with the spiritual gift of 'government'. Save, such was the extent of the damage, a plurality was called for: 'governments', I Corinthians 12:28.

Lastly, Paul names 'diversities of tongues'. That, they had in abundance, one party babbling, even shouting as if in Babel–none hearing or understanding the other–one party ranting unintelligibly in contention against another. And *this* they seemed to consider the best gift, and the one most desired by all? Yet what they put first, the apostle puts last, *after* helps and governments.

Besides, Paul calls tongues a *sign*, and a sign for those *outside the ecclesia*; not *a gift for those inside it*. See I Corinthians 14:21-25. Paul does not forbid to speak in tongues, no. But he makes an absolute condition of doing so *that another must thereafter give the interpretation*, I Corinthians 14:27,28. But how can one supposedly speaking in tongues *know beforehand* whether another will interpret or not? He *cannot* know. *Then* what?

Besides this, no more than two or at most three should speak in or by *any* identical gift, I Corinthians 14:27-29. Moreover, not only must no woman speak in tongues in the *ecclesia*, no woman must speak *at all* in the *ecclesia*, I Corinthians 14:33-40. But which sect, denomination, apostasy, independency, or division has not broken bounds and forsaken the foundation over this?

And yet for all that, how gentle; how kind; how encouraged to *expect* their acceptance of correction–despite everything– how much in remembrance of their wonderful beginnings, the apostle shows himself to be–full of the love of Christ, withal in righteousness–abiding steadfastly in faith, hope and love. Neither was he to be disappointed, II Corinthians 7:9-11.

Such is the fruitfulness and blessing of the *domata*, the gifts of Christ to the body, especially in that of the apostle: that perfect unity, in heart and speech, in judgment and deference, I say, perfect unity, the unity of one body, was restored. The gifts of the Spirit harmonized in one, and grace reigned through righteousness unto eternal life, whilst truth and peace pervaded throughout the entire *ecclesia*.

V

Seven Questions on the Gifts

IN closing this part of the epistle, Paul asks – to set them pondering – seven questions. In a way these questions bring together the gifts of Christ *to* the body, and the gifts of the Spirit *in* the body, I Corinthians 12:29,30.

In what way? In that, if pondered, the questions yield a price-less truth. All that is given from heaven; all that is bestowed on earth; all is to purpose. Divine purpose. And that purpose is *one*. Let the Corinthians consider it.

'Are all apostles?' No. There are twelve apostles. There were eleven. During the time after the ascension, whilst they were to wait for the coming of the Spirit, before he came – neither the Lord nor the Spirit being present; nor any such notion commanded – the eleven cast lots – *cast lots?* – for a twelfth apostle, as it were at the fall of a dice! But *afterwards* the Lord chose – who alone *could* choose – the twelfth from heaven.

Twelve apostles and no more. Their names are in the foundations of the walls of the city, Revelation 21:14.

The apostolic witnesses were entrusted with the revelation. They set forth the same in writing. That is the new testament. There is no appeal from this, no exceptions to it, and nothing can be added thereto. It is absolute: by it from Christ in heaven the apostles were sent to preach and teach the evangel and *thus* to establish the *ecclesia*. That is no *ecclesia* which is not so established. However large or venerable, it is a sham: a fraud.

The word committed unto the apostles is the foundation, of which Christ himself is the chief corner stone. There is no other, and there can be no other.

'Are all prophets?' No they certainly are not, Paul, neither would the vast majority have the faintest inkling of the *cost*, experimentally, doctrinally, and devotionally, neither of the years and decades of the suffering affliction and spiritual discipline which preceded the appearing of such *domata*.

Take John the Baptist for an example, to whose prophetic witness the Lord bore such a great testimony, John 5:35; John 3:5; I John 5:6. 'He was in the deserts till the day of his showing unto Israel', Luke 1:80. Oh? And how long was he *there*? And what did he *do* over those decades?

Let those who talk so glibly about 'prophets' answer *these* questions, and they may *just* begin to understand why, in his decade and a half of preparation, the Lord said of Paul, for example, 'I will show him how great things he must suffer for my name's sake'. As to John, no wonder that 'all men counted John, that he was a prophet indeed', Mark 11:32.

Nor would so many discount the prophets sent of the Lord under the old testament, as it is this day. But these prophesied of Christ. Of David, being a prophet, Peter testified, declaring that he foresaw Christ being raised from the dead: 'He seeing this before spake of the resurrection of Christ', Acts 2:31.

And of Christ, his sufferings and glory, spake all the prophets, Isaiah, Jeremiah, Ezekiel, Daniel, Hosea, Joel, Amos, Obadiah, Jonah, Micah, Nahum, Habakkuk, Zephaniah, Haggai, Zechariah, Malachi, and many others withal, not to mention that Moses also wrote of Christ, John 5:46,47.

Hence Christ preaches *from these* of the new testament, the evangel, saying, 'O fools, and slow of heart to believe all that the prophets have spoken: ought not Christ to have suffered these things, and to enter into his glory? And beginning at Moses and *all the prophets*, he expounded unto them in all the scriptures the things concerning himself', Luke 24:25-27.

The unique gift of the prophets continued after the sending of the apostles: 'And in these days came prophets from Jerusalem unto Antioch', Acts 11:27. 'And Judas and Silas, being prophets also themselves, exhorted the brethren', Acts 15:32. 'There came down from Judea a certain prophet, named Agabus', Acts 21:10. And what of the two mystical prophets in Revelation 11:3,4?

With so great a cloud of witnesses, is it any wonder that Paul declares of the *ecclesia* of God, concerning the mystery of Christ, 'Which in other ages was not made known unto the sons of men, as it is now revealed unto his holy apostles and prophets by the Spirit', Ephesians 3:4,5?

Moreover as to the old testament prophets Peter testifies, 'Unto whom it was revealed, that not unto themselves, but *unto us* they did minister the things, which are now reported unto you by them that have preached the evangel unto you with the Holy Ghost sent down from heaven', I Peter 1:12.

Hence the apostle Paul concludes, 'Now therefore ye are no more strangers and foreigners, but fellowcitizens with the saints, and of the household of God: *and are built upon the foundation of the apostles and prophets,* Jesus Christ himself being the chief corner stone', Ephesians 2:19,20.

Whereas it is unquestionable that–particularly following the ascension–the apostles and prophets mentioned above constitute those of the *domata* sent from heaven by the Lord of glory, nevertheless *the gift* of prophecy was and is also raised up by the Holy Ghost on earth under the same new testament, being bestowed upon chosen members of the body according to his own will. For example, from such charismatic members 'the prophecies'–note the plurality–'went before' upon Timothy, I Timothy 1:18.

Furthermore Philip the evangelist, whose house was at Caesarea, was one of the seven upon whom the apostles' hands had been laid. 'And the same man had four daughters, virgins, which did prophesy', Acts 21:9, where without doubt this refers to the *charisma* bestowed upon them.

Likewise the word to the assembled *ecclesia*, 'Let the prophets speak'– here, those members of the body on whom the Spirit had bestowed the gift–'two or three, *and let the other judge.* If anything be revealed to another that sitteth by, let the first *hold his peace.* For ye may all prophesy'–who *can* prophesy–'*one by one,* that all may learn, and all may be comforted', I Corinthians 14:29-31.

The prophet, and the gift of prophecy, opens what was hidden. Prophets have openings into the revelation, and can uncover from the sum delivered by the apostles. So that although the word was there, the meaning was hidden, but by prophecy it was uncovered.

That is, what had been once delivered to the saints was uncovered, not to say applied by the Holy Ghost and with power to effect conviction. Moreover the prophets–more or less–made known the mind and will of God, each in their own generation.

'Are all teachers?' As with the previous question concerning the prophets, just as the prophet may be either a gift of Christ from heaven or else prophecy may be a gift of the Spirit on earth, so it is with teachers and teaching. It is not that Paul is blurring the distinction: quite deliberately he is drawing out an important matter of fact.

In Ephesians 4:11 prophets are the second *doma*; but in Romans 12:6 prophecy is the first *charisma*. The first is from Christ ascended to the body, and stands in the heavenly gift of the person of the prophet; the second is from the Spirit descended in the body, and resides in the spiritual gift bestowed upon persons on earth.

Likewise Ephesians 4:11 reveals that the teachers–together with pastors–themselves are the fourth of the *doma* given from Christ in glory, whereas in Romans 12:7 'he that teacheth', as a member of the body, is given this supernatural gift of the Spirit abiding in the body upon earth–namely, the *charisma*–as 'having then gifts'– *charismata* – 'differing according to the grace that is given to us', Romans 12:5,6.

From which it is to be observed that the apostle–in challenging whether *all* had the selfsame ministry–names gifts: whether persons, or that which is bestowed upon persons, either of *domata* and *charismata*–for all their differences in origin, ability, and character–*had every single one of the brethren but one and the same gift?*

'Are all teachers?' No, but there *are* teachers in each assembly, and there *are* teachers of the assembly. So with prophets and prophecy. In either case the gift may be of the character of *doma* or that of *charisma*. Yet this dichotomy introduces a lesson to which the apostle is leading: the *divine objective* in giving *any* gifts–of whatever character–answers to a *common end, whatever* the nature of the gifts. It is to fulfil an *eternal purpose.*

Teachers? They recall the apostolic doctrine. They bring to remembrance the prophecy. They do not originate, but by the Lord from heaven, or from the Spirit on earth, they reiterate. Their gift is to repeat what had been opened. They 'bring to remembrance'. By the word of the Lord and by the power of the Spirit the teachers expound, enlarge, and declare what had been opened by the apostles and prophets.

Of the seven gifts about which the apostle questions the Corinthians in this place – as if to challenge them – the remaining four are without doubt *charismata*. Challenge them? Indeed, for the Corinthians conducted themselves as if what they considered to be the more spectacular and stridently vocal gifts were on the one hand common to all, and on the other as if they excluded any other gifts whatsoever.

'Are all workers of miracles?' – it should be, works of power; that is, are *all* gifts works of power? – 'Have *all* the gifts' – *charismata* – 'of healing? do *all* speak with tongues? do all interpret?', I Corinthians 12:29,30.

Do *all* speak with tongues, question six? No, of course not; any more than *all* are apostles, question one. Then why did the Corinthians behave to the contrary? They had not so learned Christ, no, nor the body of Christ. Nor would the Spirit support what was to the contrary of the apostles' doctrine. How could he? for he is the Spirit of *truth*. Indeed 'the Spirit *is* truth', I John 5:6.

As to 'interpretation', who cared about *that* among them? Every man, each party, spoke as if neither word nor reason existed above their babbling.

'But covet earnestly the best gifts', says the Authorized Version, I Corinthians 12:31, although the reader may prefer the more literal 'But be zealous of the better *charismata*'. Why? Were there worse? Necessarily, there were *less* than the *best*. And would they covet the worst?

Then these less than best must have been at least relative to the most profitable, yet the Corinthians' fleshly zeal coveted the least – or worst – above all, and at that, for the wrong reasons.

What? as if there were no other, let alone better, *charismata*? What? all covet the same one thing, and that for carnal show, babbling away in tongues which none understood but themselves, if even *they* knew what they were ranting about? For this was exactly the case with them; just as it is the case with their far more erroneous imitators to this very day.

VI

The More Excellent Way

'AND yet show I unto you a more excellent way.' And, thanks be to God, by the Spirit and through the truth, in much soul-travail with earnest prayer and fasting, through many tears, and out of a heart torn with love, *the apostle prevailed in leading them therein.*

Prevailed, yes, and more than prevailed, this great gift of Christ from heaven to the body of Christ at Corinth. So that at the last he could say with tears of joy, 'The grace of the Lord Jesus Christ, and the love of God, and the communion of the Holy Ghost, be with you *all.* Amen', II Corinthians 13:14.

Then what had happened to them? *God* had happened to them, to deliver them out of their carnal backsliding, to save them from their fleshly energy, to subdue fallen nature, to exalt Christ, to grant them submission to the truth declared so earnestly and graciously by the apostle. All that had happened.

75

And this had followed: 'Ye were made sorry after a godly manner, that ye might receive damage by us in nothing. For godly sorrow worketh repentance to salvation not to be repented of: but the sorrow of the world worketh death.

'For behold this selfsame thing, that ye sorrowed after a godly sort, what carefulness it wrought in you, yea, what clearing of yourselves, yea, what indignation, yea, what fear, yea, what vehement desire, yea, what zeal, yea, what revenge! In all things ye have approved yourselves to be clear in this matter', II Corinthians 7:9-11.

For they came to see not only their abuse of the gifts, yea, but their forcing in the flesh of one or two gifts in particular which *all* had emulated at the expense of what was *actually* proper to *each* one; and, at that, with fiery zeal and in carnal contention, abusing divine things to exalt the flesh.

Yea, more, they came to see that *all* gifts were means to an end, not an end in themselves. Whether it were the *domata*, or whether it were the *charismata*, or whether it were a relative form of the same gift in both kinds, it made no difference to the *reason* for which God had set all, be it in the body, or in the *ecclesia*.

For all in all, God had a purpose, an eternal purpose. When the gifts answered to *that*, they justified their existence, and profited by their use. And what was that eternal purpose? It was 'a more excellent way'.

It was to be made perfect in love, I John 4:17. It was that 'the love wherewith thou hast loved me may be in them'–all of them; and all of them together in unity–'and I in them', John 17:26.

It was that the body should be filled with the light, life, and love of the Head, dwelling in one in Father, Son, and Holy Ghost:

'As thou, Father, art in me, and I in thee, that they also may be one in us: that the world may believe that thou hast sent me', John 17:21.

Then of a truth every member of the body would echo from the heart and in the Spirit the words of that apostolic *doma* set apart and sent to them with the words of life and of the Spirit of God, 'that they all may be one', John 17:21.

What words of life are these? Why, those of that more excellent way: 'Though I speak with the tongues of men and of angels, and have not love, I am become as sounding brass, or a tinkling cymbal.

'And though I have the gift of prophecy, and understand all mysteries, and all knowledge; and though I have all faith, so that I could remove mountains, and have not love, I am nothing.

'And though I bestow all my goods to feed the poor, and though I give my body to be burned, and have not love, it profiteth me nothing.

'Love suffereth long, and is kind; love envieth not; love vaunteth not itself, is not puffed up, doth not behave itself unseemly, seeketh not her own, is not easily provoked, thinketh no evil; rejoiceth not in iniquity, but rejoiceth in the truth;

'Beareth all things, believeth all things, hopeth all things, endureth all things. Love never faileth: but whether there be prophecies, they shall fail; whether there be tongues, they shall cease; whether there be knowledge, it shall vanish away.

'For we know in part, and we prophesy in part. But when that which is perfect is come, then that which is in part shall be done away. When I was a child, I spake as a child, I understood as a child, I thought as a child: but when I became a man, I put away childish things.

'For now we see through a glass, darkly; but then face to face: now I know in part; but then shall I know even as also I am known.

'And now abideth faith, hope, love, these three; but the greatest of these is love.'

JOHN METCALFE

INDEX

TO OTHER PUBLICATIONS

PSALMS, HYMNS AND SPIRITUAL SONGS

Thoroughly revised second edition

THE PSALMS

OF THE

OLD TESTAMENT

The Psalms of the Old Testament, the result of years of painstaking labour, is an original translation into verse from the Authorized Version, which seeks to present the Psalms in the purest scriptural form possible for singing. Here, for the first time, divine names are rendered as and when they occur in the scripture, the distinction between LORD and Lord has been preserved, and every essential point of doctrine and experience appears with unique perception and fidelity.

The Psalms of the Old Testament is the first part of a trilogy written by John Metcalfe, the second part of which is entitled *Spiritual Songs from the Gospels*, and the last, *The Hymns of the New Testament*. These titles provide unique and accurate metrical versions of passages from the psalms, the gospels and the new testament epistles respectively, and are intended to be used together in the worship of God.

Price £2.50 (*postage extra*)
(hard-case binding, dust-jacket)
Printed, sewn and bound
by the John Metcalfe Publishing Trust
ISBN 1 870039 75 0

SPIRITUAL SONGS

FROM

THE GOSPELS

The *Spiritual Songs from the Gospels*, the result of years of painstaking labour, is an original translation into verse from the Authorized Version, which seeks to present essential parts of the gospels in the purest scriptural form possible for singing. The careful selection from Matthew, Mark, Luke, and John, set forth in metrical verse of the highest integrity, enables the singer to sing 'the word of Christ' as if from the scripture itself, 'richly and in all wisdom'; and, above all, in a way that facilitates worship in song of unprecedented fidelity.

The *Spiritual Songs from the Gospels* is the central part of a trilogy written by John Metcalfe, the first part of which is entitled *The Psalms of the Old Testament*, and the last, *The Hymns of the New Testament*. These titles provide unique and accurate metrical versions of passages from the psalms, the gospels and the new testament epistles respectively, and are intended to be used together in the worship of God.

Price £2.50 *(postage extra)*
(hard-case binding, dust-jacket)
Printed, sewn and bound
by the John Metcalfe Publishing Trust
ISBN 0 9506366 8 1

THE HYMNS

OF THE

NEW TESTAMENT

The Hymns of the New Testament, the result of years of painstaking labour, is an original translation into verse from the Authorized Version, which presents essential parts of the new testament epistles in the purest scriptural form possible for singing. The careful selection from the book of Acts to that of Revelation, set forth in metrical verse of the highest integrity, enables the singer to sing 'the word of Christ' as if from the scripture itself, 'richly and in all wisdom'; and, above all, in a way that facilitates worship in song of unprecedented fidelity.

The Hymns of the New Testament is the last part of a trilogy written by John Metcalfe, the first part of which is entitled *The Psalms of the Old Testament*, and the next, *Spiritual Songs from the Gospels*. These titles provide unique and accurate metrical versions of passages from the psalms, the gospels and the new testament epistles respectively, and are intended to be used together in the worship of God.

Price £2.50 *(postage extra)*
(hard-case binding, dust-jacket)
Printed, sewn and bound
by the John Metcalfe Publishing Trust
ISBN 0 9506366 9 X

'THE APOSTOLIC FOUNDATION
OF THE
CHRISTIAN CHURCH' SERIES

x

Third Printing

FOUNDATIONS UNCOVERED

THE APOSTOLIC FOUNDATION
OF THE
CHRISTIAN CHURCH

Volume I

Foundations Uncovered is the introduction to the major series: 'The Apostolic Foundation of the Christian Church'.

Rich in truth, the Introduction deals comprehensively with the foundation of the apostolic faith under the descriptive titles: The Word, The Doctrine, The Truth, The Gospel, The Faith, The New Testament, and The Foundation.

The contents of the book reveal: The Fact of the Foundation; The Foundation Uncovered; What the Foundation is not; How the Foundation is Described; and, Being Built upon the Foundation.

'This book comes with the freshness of a new Reformation.'

Price 75p (*postage extra*)
Paperback 110 pages (Laminated cover)
Printed, sewn and bound
by the John Metcalfe Publishing Trust
ISBN 0 9506366 5 7

Thoroughly revised and extensively rewritten second edition

Third Printing

THE BIRTH OF JESUS CHRIST

THE APOSTOLIC FOUNDATION
OF THE
CHRISTIAN CHURCH

Volume II

Price 95p (*postage extra*)
Paperback 160 pages (Laminated cover)
Printed, sewn and bound
by the John Metcalfe Publishing Trust
ISBN 1 870039 48 3

*Thoroughly revised and extensively rewritten
second edition (Hardback)*

Third Printing

THE MESSIAH

THE APOSTOLIC FOUNDATION
OF THE
CHRISTIAN CHURCH

Volume III

The Messiah is a spiritually penetrating and entirely original
exposition of Matthew chapter one to chapter seven from the
trenchant pen of John Metcalfe.

Matthew Chapters One to Seven

GENEALOGY · BIRTH · STAR OF BETHLEHEM
HEROD · FLIGHT TO EGYPT · NAZARETH
JOHN THE BAPTIST · THE BAPTIST'S MINISTRY
JESUS' BAPTISM · ALL RIGHTEOUSNESS FULFILLED
HEAVEN OPENED · THE SPIRIT'S DESCENT
THE TEMPTATION OF JESUS IN THE WILDERNESS
JESUS' MANIFESTATION · THE CALLING · THE TRUE DISCIPLES
THE BEATITUDES · THE SERMON ON THE MOUNT

'Something of the fire of the ancient Hebrew prophet ......
Metcalfe has spiritual and expository potentials of a high order.'
The Life of Faith.

Price £7.75 (*postage extra*)
Hardback 420 pages
Laminated bookjacket
Printed, sewn and bound
by the John Metcalfe Publishing Trust
ISBN 1 870039 51 3

Second Edition (Hardback)

THE SON OF GOD AND SEED OF DAVID

THE APOSTOLIC FOUNDATION
OF THE
CHRISTIAN CHURCH

Volume IV

The Son of God and Seed of David is the fourth volume in the major work entitled 'The Apostolic Foundation of the Christian Church'.

'The Author proceeds to open and allege that Jesus Christ is and ever was *The Son of God*. This greatest of subjects, this most profound of all mysteries, is handled with reverence and with outstanding perception.

'The second part considers *The Seed of David*. What is meant precisely by 'the seed'? And why 'of David'? With prophetic insight the author expounds these essential verities.

Price £6.95 (*postage extra*)
Hardback 250 pages
Laminated bookjacket
Printed, sewn and bound
by the John Metcalfe Publishing Trust
ISBN 1 870039 16 5

CHRIST CRUCIFIED

THE APOSTOLIC FOUNDATION
OF THE
CHRISTIAN CHURCH

Volume V

Christ Crucified, the definitive work on the crucifixion, the blood, and the cross of Jesus Christ.

The crucifixion of Jesus Christ witnessed in the Gospels: the gospel according to Matthew; Mark; Luke; John.

The blood of Jesus Christ declared in the Epistles: the shed blood; the blood of purchase; redemption through his blood; the blood of sprinkling; the blood of the covenant.

The doctrine of the cross revealed in the apostolic foundation of the Christian church: the doctrine of the cross; the cross and the body of sin; the cross and the carnal mind; the cross and the law; the offence of the cross; the cross of our Lord Jesus Christ.

Price £6.95 (*postage extra*)
Hardback 300 pages
Laminated bookjacket
Printed, sewn and bound
by the John Metcalfe Publishing Trust
ISBN 1 870039 08 4

JUSTIFICATION BY FAITH

THE APOSTOLIC FOUNDATION
OF THE
CHRISTIAN CHURCH

Volume VI

THE HEART OF THE GOSPEL · THE FOUNDATION OF THE CHURCH
THE ISSUE OF ETERNITY
CLEARLY, ORIGINALLY AND POWERFULLY OPENED

The basis · The righteousness of the law
The righteousness of God · The atonement · Justification
Traditional views considered · Righteousness imputed to faith
Faith counted for righteousness · Justification by Faith

'And it came to pass, when Jesus had ended these sayings, the people
were astonished at his doctrine: for he taught them as one having
authority, and not as the scribes', Matthew 7:28,29.

Price £7.50 (postage extra)
Hardback 375 pages
Laminated bookjacket
Printed, sewn and bound
by the John Metcalfe Publishing Trust
ISBN 1 870039 11 4

THE CHURCH: WHAT IS IT?

THE APOSTOLIC FOUNDATION
OF THE
CHRISTIAN CHURCH

Volume VII

The answer to this question proceeds first from the lips of Jesus himself, Mt. 16:18, later to be expounded by the words of the apostles whom he sent.

Neither fear of man nor favour from the world remotely affect the answer.

Here is the truth, the whole truth, and nothing but the truth.

The complete originality, the vast range, and the total fearlessness of this book command the attention in a way that is unique.

Read this book: you will never read another like it.

Outspokenly devastating yet devastatingly constructive.

Price £7.75 (*postage extra*)
Hardback 400 pages
Laminated bookjacket
Printed, sewn and bound
by the John Metcalfe Publishing Trust
ISBN 1 870039 23 8

THE REVELATION OF JESUS CHRIST

THE APOSTOLIC FOUNDATION
OF THE
CHRISTIAN CHURCH

Volume VIII

Uniquely perceptive and original, the result of decades alone in the secret place of the most High, abiding under the shadow of the Almighty, this peerless work on the Revelation of Jesus Christ will stand the test of time and eternity for its heavenly, spiritual, and divine opening into the last book of the last apostle of the new testament, for all who have an ear to hear what the Spirit saith unto the churches.

Here is the transcript of the series of addresses delivered over some eighteen months during 1997 and 1998, in the Assembly Hall, Church House, Westminster, London, by John Metcalfe.

The famed Assembly Hall is used as the Synod Chamber of the Church of England as occasion requires.

Price £9.25 (*postage extra*)
Hardback 640 pages
Laminated bookjacket
Printed, sewn and bound
by the John Metcalfe Publishing Trust
ISBN 1 870039 77 7

LECTURES
FROM
CHURCH HOUSE, WESTMINSTER

COLOSSIANS

This concise and unique revelation of the Epistle to the Colossians has the hallmark of spiritual originality and insight peculiar to the ministry of John Metcalfe. It is as if a diamond, inert and lifeless in itself, has been divinely cut at great cost, so that every way in which it is turned, the light from above is enhanced and magnified to break forth with divine radiance showing colour and depth hitherto unsuspected.

Price 95p *(postage extra)*
Paperback 135 pages (Laminated cover)
Printed, sewn and bound
by the John Metcalfe Publishing Trust
ISBN 1 870039 55 6

MATTHEW

This concise revelation of the essence and structure of the Gospel according to Matthew, the culmination of years of prayer and devotion, retreat and study, opens the mind of the Spirit in the unique vision of Jesus Christ, the son of David, the son of Abraham, recorded in the first gospel.

Price 95p *(postage extra)*
Paperback 135 pages (Laminated cover)
Printed, sewn and bound
by the John Metcalfe Publishing Trust
ISBN 1 870039 61 0

PHILIPPIANS

The Epistle of Paul the Apostle to the Philippians is opened by this work from the pen of John Metcalfe with that lucid thoroughness which one has come to expect from a ministry received 'not of men, neither by man, but by the revelation of Jesus Christ'.

The work of God at Philippi is traced 'from the first day' until the time at which the epistle was written. Never was Lydia or the Philippian jailor drawn with more lively insight. The epistle itself is revealed in order, with passages–such as 'the mind that was in Christ Jesus'–that evidence the work of no less than a divine for our own times.

Price £1.90 (*postage extra*)
Paperback 185 pages (Laminated cover)
Printed, sewn and bound
by the John Metcalfe Publishing Trust
ISBN 1 870039 56 4

PHILEMON

This penetrating revelation of the Epistle to Philemon opens the substance of four consecutive lectures given by John Metcalfe in The Hoare Memorial Hall, Church House, Westminster, London.

Price £1.90 (*postage extra*)
Paperback 190 pages (Laminated cover)
Printed, sewn and bound
by the John Metcalfe Publishing Trust
ISBN 1 870039 66 1

FIRST TIMOTHY

This penetrating revelation of the First Epistle to Timothy opens the substance of five consecutive lectures given by John Metcalfe in The Hoare Memorial Hall, Church House, Westminster, London.

Price £2.00 (*postage extra*)
Paperback 220 pages (Laminated cover)
Printed, sewn and bound
by the John Metcalfe Publishing Trust
ISBN 1 870039 67 X

MARK

This penetrating revelation of the Gospel according to Mark opens the substance of seven consecutive lectures given by John Metcalfe in The Hoare Memorial Hall, Church House, Westminster, London.

Price £2.35 (*postage extra*)
Paperback 290 pages (Laminated cover)
Printed, sewn and bound
by the John Metcalfe Publishing Trust
ISBN 1 870039 70 X

Third Printing

CREATION

Genesis 1:1, 'In the beginning God created the heaven and the earth.'

This spiritually penetrating and outstandingly original revelation of the Creation from Genesis chapters 1 and 2 opens the substance of five consecutive lectures given by John Metcalfe, commencing in the Hoare Memorial Hall and later moving to the central Assembly Hall, Church House, Westminster, London.

The Hoare Memorial Hall was used as the House of Commons at various times during the Second World War. Many of Sir Winston Churchill's renowned war time speeches were delivered in this Hall.

The famed Assembly Hall is used as the Synod Chamber of the Church of England as occasion requires.

Price £2.00 *(postage extra)*
Paperback 230 pages (Laminated cover)
Printed, sewn and bound
by the John Metcalfe Publishing Trust
ISBN 1 870039 71 8

NEWLY PUBLISHED

THE FIRST EPISTLE OF JOHN

Deeply spiritual and of the very essence, it is as if one heard
the apostle himself taking and opening the book in a way that
is unprecedented.

THE BEGINNING . THE MESSAGE . THE COMMANDMENTS
THE LITTLE CHILDREN . THE ABIDING
THE WITNESS . THE CONCLUSION

Price £9.25 (*postage extra*)
Hardback 585 pages
Laminated bookjacket
Printed, sewn and bound
by the John Metcalfe Publishing Trust
ISBN 1 870039 78 5

OTHER TITLES

Second Edition
Fourth Printing

NOAH AND THE FLOOD

Noah and the Flood expounds with vital urgency the man and the message that heralded the end of the old world. The description of the flood itself is vividly realistic. The whole work has an unmistakable ring of authority, and speaks as 'Thus saith the Lord'.

'Mr. Metcalfe makes a skilful use of persuasive eloquence as he challenges the reality of one's profession of faith ... he gives a rousing call to a searching self-examination and evaluation of one's spiritual experience.'

The Monthly Record of the Free Church of Scotland.

Price £1.90 (*postage extra*)
Paperback 155 pages (Laminated cover)
Printed, sewn and bound
by the John Metcalfe Publishing Trust
ISBN 1 870039 22 X

DIVINE FOOTSTEPS

Divine Footsteps traces the pathway of the feet of the Son of man from the very beginning in the prophetic figures of the true in the old testament through the reality in the new; doing so in a way of experimental spirituality. At the last a glimpse of the coming glory is beheld as his feet are viewed as standing at the latter day upon the earth.

Price 95p (*postage extra*)
Paperback 120 pages (Laminated cover)
Printed, sewn and bound by
the John Metcalfe Publishing Trust
ISBN 1 870039 21 1

THE RED HEIFER

The Red Heifer was the name given to a sacrifice used by the children of Israel in the Old Testament – as recorded in Numbers 19 – in which a heifer was slain and burned. Cedar wood, hyssop and scarlet were cast into the burning, and the ashes were mingled with running water and put in a vessel. It was kept for the children of Israel for a water of separation: it was a purification for sin.

In this unusual book the sacrifice is brought up to date and its relevance to the church today is shown.

Price 75p (*postage extra*)
Paperback 100 pages
ISBN 0 9502515 4 2

OF GOD OR MAN?

LIGHT FROM GALATIANS

The Epistle to the Galatians contends for deliverance from the law and from carnal ministry.

The Apostle opens his matter in two ways:

Firstly, Paul vindicates himself and his ministry against those that came not from God above, but from Jerusalem below.

Secondly, he defends the Gospel and evangelical liberty against legal perversions and bondage to the flesh.

Price £1.45 (*postage extra*)
Paperback 190 pages (Laminated cover)
ISBN 0 9506366 3 0

THE BOOK OF RUTH

The Book of Ruth is set against the farming background of old testament Israel at the time of the Judges, the narrative – unfolding the work of God in redemption – being marked by a series of agricultural events.

These events – the famine; the barley harvest; the wheat harvest; the winnowing – possessed a hidden spiritual significance to that community, but, much more, they speak in figure directly to our own times, as the book reveals.

Equally contemporary appear the characters of Ruth, Naomi, Boaz, and the first kinsman, drawn with spiritual perception greatly to the profit of the reader.

Price £4.95 (*postage extra*)
Hardback 200 pages
Laminated bookjacket
Printed, sewn and bound
by the John Metcalfe Publishing Trust
ISBN 1 870039 17 3

A QUESTION FOR POPE JOHN PAUL II

As a consequence of his many years spent apart in prayer, lonely vigil, and painstaking study of the scripture, John Metcalfe asks a question and looks for an answer from Pope John Paul II.

Price £1.25 (*postage extra*)
Paperback 105 pages (Laminated cover)
ISBN 0 9506366 4 9

DIVINE MEDITATIONS

OF

WILLIAM HUNTINGTON

Originally published by Mr. Huntington as a series of letters to J. Jenkins, under the title of 'Contemplations on the God of Israel', the spiritual content of this correspondence has been skilfully and sympathetically edited, abridged, and arranged so as to form a series of meditations, suitable for daily readings.

Mr. Huntington's own text is thereby adapted to speak directly to the reader in a way much more suited to his ministering immediately to ourselves, in our own circumstances and times.

It is greatly hoped that many today will benefit from this adaption which carefully retains both the spirit and the letter of the text. If any prefer the original format, this is readily available from several sources and many libraries.

Nevertheless, the publishers believe the much more readable form into which Mr. Huntington's very words have been adapted will appeal to a far wider audience, for whose comfort and consolation this carefully edited work has been published.

Price £2.35 (*postage extra*)
Paperback 300 pages (Laminated cover)
Printed, sewn and bound
by the John Metcalfe Publishing Trust
ISBN 1 870039 24 6

Second Edition

Third Printing

THE WELLS OF SALVATION

The Wells of Salvation is written from a series of seven powerful addresses preached at Tylers Green. It is a forthright and experimental exposition of Isaiah 12:3, 'Therefore with joy shall ye draw water out of the wells of salvation.'

John Metcalfe is acknowledged to be perhaps the most gifted expositor and powerful preacher of our day and this is to be seen clearly in The Wells of Salvation.

Price £2.35 *(postage extra)*
Paperback 285 pages (Laminated cover)
Printed, sewn and bound
by the John Metcalfe Publishing Trust
ISBN 1 870039 72 6

Second Printing

SAVING FAITH

The sevenfold work of the Holy Ghost in bringing a sinner to saving faith in Christ opened and enlarged.

True faith is the work of God. False faith is the presumption of man. But where is the difference? *Saving Faith* shows the difference.

Price £2.25 *(postage extra)*
Paperback 250 pages (Laminated cover)
Printed, sewn and bound
by the John Metcalfe Publishing Trust
ISBN 1 870039 40 8

DELIVERANCE FROM THE LAW
THE WESTMINSTER CONFESSION EXPLODED

Deliverance from the Law. A devastating vindication of the gospel of Christ against the traditions of man.

Price £1.90 (*postage extra*)
Paperback 160 pages (Laminated cover)
Printed, sewn and bound
by the John Metcalfe Publishing Trust
ISBN 1 870039 41 6

PRESENT-DAY CONVERSIONS
OF THE NEW TESTAMENT KIND

FROM THE MINISTRY OF
JOHN METCALFE

The outstandingly striking presentation of this fascinating paperback will surely catch the eye, as its title and contents will certainly captivate the mind: here is a unique publication.

Woven into a gripping narrative, over twenty-one short life stories, all centred on conversions that simply could not have happened had not God broken in, and had not Christ been revealed, the book presents a tremendous challenge, at once moving and thrilling to the reader.

Price £2.25 (*postage extra*)
Paperback 240 pages (Laminated cover)
Printed, sewn and bound
by the John Metcalfe Publishing Trust
ISBN 1 870039 31 9

THE BEATITUDES

A unique insight destined to be the classic opening of this wonderful sequence of utterances from the lips of Jesus.

The reader will discover a penetration of the spiritual heights and divine depths of these peerless words in a way ever fresh and always rewarding though read time and time again.

Price £1.90 (*postage extra*)
Paperback 185 pages (Laminated cover)
Printed, sewn and bound
by the John Metcalfe Publishing Trust
ISBN 1 870039 45 9

PASTORAL LETTERS TO THE FAR EAST

Feeling the abiding spiritual value of letters written by John Metcalfe in his absence from the Far East, Miss Sie Siok Hui cherished the correspondence to her, and at the same time was moved to seek for similar writings to some of her closest sisters in Christ.

Gathering these letters together, it was her earnest desire that such an enduring testimony should be made available to all the faithful remnant in our own day. The result of her prayers and spiritual exercise appears in the publication 'Pastoral Letters to the Far East'.

Price £2.00 (*postage extra*)
Paperback 240 pages (Laminated cover)
Printed, sewn and bound
by the John Metcalfe Publishing Trust
ISBN 1 870039 74 2

LAW AND GRACE CONTRASTED

A SERIES OF ADDRESSES

BY

WILLIAM HUNTINGTON

The Child of Liberty in Legal Bondage · The Bondchild
brought to the Test · The Modern Plasterer Detected
Not under Law · The Law a Rule of Life?

Mr. Huntington's own text is adapted to speak directly to the
reader in a way much more suited to his ministering immediately to ourselves, in our own circumstances and times.

It is greatly hoped that many today will benefit from this
adaption which carefully retains both the spirit and the letter
of the text. If any prefer the original format, this is readily
available from several sources and many libraries.

Nevertheless, the publishers believe the much more readable
form into which Mr. Huntington's very words have been
adapted will appeal to a far wider audience, for whose comfort
and consolation this carefully edited work has been published.

Price £2.35 (*postage extra*)
Paperback 265 pages (Laminated cover)
Printed, sewn and bound
by the John Metcalfe Publishing Trust
ISBN 1 870039 76 9

NEWLY PUBLISHED

THE GIFTS AND BAPTISM
OF THE SPIRIT

For so long confusion has reigned in respect of THE GIFTS AND
BAPTISM OF THE SPIRIT. Here at last is that spiritual, sound, and
balanced opening of the Holy Scripture from I Corinthians
12:1-13.

This gives the unmistakable ring of apostolic authority, puts
the matter beyond the realm of speculation or experiment,
past all doubt bringing the text into the light of revelation of
Jesus Christ.

Price 95p (*postage extra*)
Paperback 128 pages (Laminated cover)
Printed, sewn and bound
by the John Metcalfe Publishing Trust
ISBN 1 870039 80 7

'TRACT FOR THE TIMES' SERIES

'TRACT FOR THE TIMES' SERIES

The Gospel of God by John Metcalfe. No. 1 in the Series. Laminated cover, price 25p.

The Strait Gate by John Metcalfe. No. 2 in the Series. Laminated cover, price 25p.

Eternal Sonship and Taylor Brethren by John Metcalfe. No. 3 in the Series. Laminated cover, price 25p.

Marks of the New Testament Church by John Metcalfe. No. 4 in the Series. Laminated cover, price 25p.

The Charismatic Delusion by John Metcalfe. No. 5 in the Series. Laminated cover, price 25p.

Premillennialism Exposed by John Metcalfe. No. 6 in the Series. Laminated cover, price 25p.

Justification and Peace by John Metcalfe. No. 7 in the Series. Laminated cover, price 25p.

Faith or Presumption? by John Metcalfe. No. 8 in the Series. Laminated cover, price 25p.

The Elect Undeceived by John Metcalfe. No. 9 in the Series. Laminated cover, price 25p.

Justifying Righteousness by John Metcalfe. No. 10 in the Series. Laminated cover, price 25p.

Righteousness Imputed by John Metcalfe. No. 11 in the Series. Laminated cover, price 25p.

The Great Deception by John Metcalfe. No. 12 in the Series. Laminated cover, price 25p.

A Famine in the Land by John Metcalfe. No. 13 in the Series. Laminated cover, price 25p.

Blood and Water by John Metcalfe. No. 14 in the Series. Laminated cover, price 25p.

Women Bishops? by John Metcalfe. No. 15 in the Series. Laminated cover, price 25p.

The Heavenly Vision by John Metcalfe. No. 16 in the Series. Laminated cover, price 25p.

EVANGELICAL TRACTS

EVANGELICAL TRACTS

1. **The Two Prayers of Elijah.** Light green card cover, price 10p.

2. **Wounded for our Transgressions.** Gold card cover, price 10p.

3. **The Blood of Sprinkling.** Red card cover, price 10p.

4. **The Grace of God that brings Salvation.** Blue card cover, price 10p.

5. **The Name of Jesus.** Rose card cover, price 10p.

6. **The Ministry of the New Testament.** Purple card cover, price 10p.

7. **The Death of the Righteous** (*The closing days of J.B. Stoney*) by A.M.S. (his daughter). Ivory card cover, price 10p.

8. **Repentance.** Sky blue card cover, price 10p.

9. **Legal Deceivers Exposed.** Crimson card cover, price 10p.

10. **Unconditional Salvation.** Green card cover, price 10p.

11. **Religious Merchandise.** Brown card cover, price 10p.

12. **Comfort.** Pink card cover, price 10p.

13. **Peace.** Grey card cover, price 10p.

14. **Eternal Life.** Cobalt card cover, price 10p.

15. **The Handwriting of Ordinances.** Fawn card cover, price 10p.

16. **'Lord, Lord!'.** Emerald card cover, price 10p.

17. **Conversion.** Wedgewood card cover, price 10p.

ECCLESIA TRACTS

ECCLESIA TRACTS

The Beginning of the Ecclesia by John Metcalfe. No. 1 in the Series, Sand grain cover, price 10p.

Churches and the Church by J.N. Darby. Edited. No. 2 in the Series, Sand grain cover, price 10p.

The Ministers of Christ by John Metcalfe. No. 3 in the Series, Sand grain cover, price 10p.

The Inward Witness by George Fox. Edited. No. 4 in the Series, Sand grain cover, price 10p.

The Notion of a Clergyman by J.N. Darby. Edited. No. 5 in the Series, Sand grain cover, price 10p.

The Servant of the Lord by William Huntington. Edited and Abridged. No. 6 in the Series, Sand grain cover, price 10p.

One Spirit by William Kelly. Edited. No. 7 in the Series, Sand grain cover, price 10p.

The Funeral of Arminianism by William Huntington. Edited and Abridged. No. 8 in the Series, Sand grain cover, price 10p.

One Body by William Kelly. Edited. No. 9 in the Series, Sand grain cover, price 10p.

False Churches and True by John Metcalfe. No. 10 in the Series, Sand grain cover, price 10p.

Separation from Evil by J.N. Darby. Edited. No. 11 in the Series, Sand grain cover, price 10p.

The Remnant by J.B. Stoney. Edited. No. 12 in the Series, Sand grain cover, price 10p.

The Arminian Skeleton by William Huntington. Edited and Abridged. No. 13 in the Series, Sand grain cover, price 10p.

FOUNDATION TRACTS

FOUNDATION TRACTS

1. **Female Priests?** by John Metcalfe. Oatmeal cover, price 25p.

2. **The Bondage of the Will** by Martin Luther. Translated and Abridged. Oatmeal cover, price 25p.

3. **Of the Popish Mass** by John Calvin. Translated and Abridged. Oatmeal cover, price 25p.

4. **The Adversary** by John Metcalfe. Oatmeal cover, price 25p.

5. **The Advance of Popery** by J.C. Philpot. Oatmeal cover, price 25p.

6. **Enemies in the Land** by John Metcalfe. Oatmeal cover, price 25p.

7. **An Admonition Concerning Relics** by John Calvin. Oatmeal cover, price 25p.

8. **John Metcalfe's Testimony Against Falsity in Worship** by John Metcalfe. Oatmeal cover, price 25p.

9. **Brethrenism Exposed** by John Metcalfe. Oatmeal cover, price 25p.

10. **John Metcalfe's Testimony Against The Social Gospel** by John Metcalfe. Oatmeal cover, price 25p.

MINISTRY BY JOHN METCALFE

TAPE MINISTRY BY JOHN METCALFE
FROM THE U.K. AND THE FAR EAST
IS AVAILABLE

In order to obtain this free recorded ministry, please send your blank cassette (C.90) and the cost of the return postage, including your name and address in block capitals, to the John Metcalfe Publishing Trust, Church Road, Tylers Green, Penn, Bucks, HP10 8LN. Tapelists are available on request.

Owing to the increased demand for the tape ministry, we are unable to supply more than two tapes per order, except in the case of meetings for the hearing of tapes, where a special arrangement can be made.

THE MINISTRY OF THE NEW TESTAMENT

The purpose of this substantial A4 gloss paper magazine is to provide spiritual and experimental ministry with sound doctrine which rightly and prophetically divides the word of truth.

Readers of our books will already know the high standards of our publications. They can be confident that these pages will maintain that quality, by giving access to enduring ministry from the past, much of which is derived from sources that are virtually unobtainable today, and publishing a living ministry from the present. Selected articles from the following writers have already been included:

ELI ASHDOWN · JOHN BERRIDGE · ABRAHAM BOOTH
JOHN BRADFORD · JOHN BUNYAN · JOHN BURGON
JOHN CALVIN · DONALD CARGILL · JOHN CENNICK · J.N. DARBY
GEORGE FOX · JOHN FOXE · WILLIAM GADSBY · JOHN GUTHRIE
WILLIAM GUTHRIE · GREY HAZLERIGG · WILLIAM HUNTINGTON
WILLIAM KELLY · JOHN KENNEDY · JOHN KERSHAW
JOHN KEYT · HANSERD KNOLLYS · JOHN KNOX · JAMES LEWIS
MARTIN LUTHER · ROBERT MURRAY MCCHEYNE · JOHN METCALFE
BROWNLOW NORTH · THOMAS OXENHAM · ALEXANDER–SANDY–PEDEN
J.C. PHILPOT · J.K. POPHAM · JAMES RENWICK · J.B. STONEY
HENRY TANNER · ARTHUR TRIGGS · JOHN VINALL · JOHN WARBURTON
JOHN WELWOOD · GEORGE WHITEFIELD · J.A. WYLIE

Price £1.75 (*postage included*)
Issued Spring, Summer, Autumn, Winter.

Magazine Order Form

Name and address (in block capitals)

....

....

....

cut here

Please send me ...... current copy/copies of The Ministry of the New Testament.

Please send me ...... year/s subscription.

I enclose a cheque/postal order for £......

(Price: including postage, U.K. £1.75; Overseas £1.90)
(One year's subscription: including postage, U.K. £7.00; Overseas £7.60)

Cheques should be made payable to The John Metcalfe Publishing Trust, and for overseas subscribers should be in pounds sterling drawn on a London Bank.

10 or more copies to one address will qualify for a 10% discount.

Some back numbers from Spring 1986 available.

Please send to The John Metcalfe Publishing Trust, Church Road, Tylers Green, Penn, Bucks, HP10 8LN.

All publications of the Trust are subsidised by the Publishers

lvii

Book Order Form

Please send to the address below:

	Price	Quantity
A Question for Pope John Paul II	£1.25	......
Of God or Man?	£1.45	......
Noah and the Flood	£1.90	......
Divine Footsteps	£0.95	......
The Red Heifer	£0.75	......
The Wells of Salvation	£2.35	......
The Book of Ruth (Hardback edition)	£4.95	......
Divine Meditations of William Huntington	£2.35	......
Present-Day Conversions of the New Testament Kind	£2.25	......
Saving Faith	£2.25	......
Deliverance from the Law	£1.90	......
The Beatitudes	£1.90	......
Pastoral Letters to the Far East	£2.00	......
Law and Grace Contrasted by William Huntington	£2.35	......
The Gifts and Baptism of the Spirit	£0.95	......
The Body of Christ and the Gifts	£0.95	......

Lectures from Church House, Westminster

	Price	Quantity
Colossians	£0.95	......
Philippians	£1.90	......
Matthew	£0.95	......
Philemon	£1.90	......
First Timothy	£2.00	......
Mark	£2.35	......
Creation	£2.00	......
The First Epistle of John (Hardback edition)	£9.25	......

Psalms, Hymns & Spiritual Songs (Hardback edition)

	Price	Quantity
The Psalms of the Old Testament	£2.50	......
Spiritual Songs from the Gospels	£2.50	......
The Hymns of the New Testament	£2.50	......

'Apostolic Foundation of the Christian Church' series

		Price	Quantity
Foundations Uncovered	Vol. I	£0.75	......
The Birth of Jesus Christ	Vol. II	£0.95	......
The Messiah (Hardback edition)	Vol. III	£7.75	......
The Son of God and Seed of David (Hardback edition)	Vol. IV	£6.95	......
Christ Crucified (Hardback edition)	Vol. V	£6.95	......
Justification by Faith (Hardback edition)	Vol. VI	£7.50	......
The Church: What is it? (Hardback edition)	Vol. VII	£7.75	......
The Revelation of Jesus Christ (Hardback edition)	Vol. VIII	£9.25	......

Name and address (in block capitals)

....

....

....

If money is sent with order please allow for postage. Please address to:- The
John Metcalfe Publishing Trust, Church Road, Tylers Green, Penn, Bucks, HP10 8LN.

cut here

Tract Order Form

Please send to the address below:

		Price	Quantity
Evangelical Tracts			
The Two Prayers of Elijah		£0.10	......
Wounded for our Transgressions		£0.10	......
The Blood of Sprinkling		£0.10	......
The Grace of God that brings Salvation		£0.10	......
The Name of Jesus		£0.10	......
The Ministry of the New Testament		£0.10	......
The Death of the Righteous by A.M.S.		£0.10	......
Repentance		£0.10	......
Legal Deceivers Exposed		£0.10	......
Unconditional Salvation		£0.10	......
Religious Merchandise		£0.10	......
Comfort		£0.10	......
Peace		£0.10	......
Eternal Life		£0.10	......
The Handwriting of Ordinances		£0.10	......
'Lord, Lord!'		£0.10	......
Conversion		£0.10	......
'Tract for the Times' series			
The Gospel of God	No. 1	£0.25	......
The Strait Gate	No. 2	£0.25	......
Eternal Sonship and Taylor Brethren	No. 3	£0.25	......
Marks of the New Testament Church	No. 4	£0.25	......
The Charismatic Delusion	No. 5	£0.25	......
Premillennialism Exposed	No. 6	£0.25	......
Justification and Peace	No. 7	£0.25	......
Faith or Presumption?	No. 8	£0.25	......
The Elect Undeceived	No. 9	£0.25	......
Justifying Righteousness	No.10	£0.25	......
Righteousness Imputed	No.11	£0.25	......
The Great Deception	No.12	£0.25	......
A Famine in the Land	No.13	£0.25	......
Blood and Water	No.14	£0.25	......
Women Bishops?	No.15	£0.25	......
The Heavenly Vision	No.16	£0.25	......

Name and address (in block capitals)

....

....

....

If money is sent with order please allow for postage. Please address to:- The John Metcalfe Publishing Trust, Church Road, Tylers Green, Penn, Bucks, HP10 8LN.

cut here

Tract Order Form

Please send to the address below:

		Price	Quantity

Ecclesia Tracts

		Price	Quantity
The Beginning of the Ecclesia	No. 1	£0.10	......
Churches and the Church (J.N.D.)	No. 2	£0.10	......
The Ministers of Christ	No. 3	£0.10	......
The Inward Witness (G.F.)	No. 4	£0.10	......
The Notion of a Clergyman (J.N.D.)	No. 5	£0.10	......
The Servant of the Lord (W.H.)	No. 6	£0.10	......
One Spirit (W.K.)	No. 7	£0.10	......
The Funeral of Arminianism (W.H.)	No. 8	£0.10	......
One Body (W.K.)	No. 9	£0.10	......
False Churches and True	No.10	£0.10	......
Separation from Evil (J.N.D.)	No.11	£0.10	......
The Remnant (J.B.S.)	No.12	£0.10	......
The Arminian Skeleton (W.H.)	No.13	£0.10	......

Foundation Tracts

		Price	Quantity
Female Priests?	No. 1	£0.25	......
The Bondage of the Will (Martin Luther)	No. 2	£0.25	......
Of the Popish Mass (John Calvin)	No. 3	£0.25	......
The Adversary	No. 4	£0.25	......
The Advance of Popery (J.C. Philpot)	No. 5	£0.25	......
Enemies in the Land	No. 6	£0.25	......
An Admonition Concerning Relics (John Calvin)	No. 7	£0.25	......
John Metcalfe's Testimony Against Falsity in Worship	No. 8	£0.25	......
Brethrenism Exposed	No. 9	£0.25	......
John Metcalfe's Testimony Against The Social Gospel	No.10	£0.25	......

Name and address (in block capitals)

....

....

....

If money is sent with order please allow for postage. Please address to:- The John Metcalfe Publishing Trust, Church Road, Tylers Green, Penn, Bucks, HP10 8LN.

cut here